THE GREAT NEGRO PLOT

THE GREAT
NEGRO PLOT

A TALE OF CONSPIRACY AND MURDER
IN EIGHTEENTH-CENTURY NEW YORK

MAT JOHNSON

BLOOMSBURY

Published by Bloomsbury USA, New York
Distributed to the trade by Holtzbrinck Publishers

All papers used by Bloomsbury USA are natural, recyclable products made
from wood grown in well-managed forests. The manufacturing processes
conform to the environmental regulations of the country of origin.

Library of Congress Cataloging-in-Publication Data

Johnson, Mat.
The Great Negro Plot : a tale of conspiracy and murder
in eighteenth-century New York/Mat Johnson.
p. cm.
ISBN-13: 978-1-58234-099-9 (hardcover)
ISBN-10: 1-58234-099-4 (hardcover)
1. New York (N.Y.)—History—Conspiracy of 1741. 2. Slave
insurrections—New York (State)—New York—History—18th century.
3. Conspiracies—New York (State)—New York—history—18th
century. 4. Murder—New York (State)—New York—History—18th
century. 5. New York (N.Y.)—Race relations—History—18th century.
6. New York (N.Y.)—History—Colonial period, ca. 1600–1775. I. Title.
F128.4.J64 2007
974.7'02—dc22
2006034162

First U.S. Edition 2007

1   3   5   7   9   10   8   6   4   2

Typeset by Westchester Book Group
Printed in the United States of America by Quebecor World Fairfield

For Jasmin:

This is the world.

In estimating this singular event in our colonial history, the circumstances of the time should be daily considered, before we too hastily condemn the bigotry and cruelty of our predecessors. The advantages of a liberal, indeed of the plainest education, was the happy lot of very few. Intercourse between colonies and the mother country, and between province and province, was very rare. Ignorance and illiberal prejudices universally prevailed. Their more favoured and enlightened posterity will, therefore, draw the veil of filial affection over the involuntary errors of their forefathers, and emulating their simple virtues, endeavour to transmit a brighter example to their successors.

—Anonymous, Introduction,
The New York Conspiracy, 1810 Edition
(New York: Southwick & Pelsue, April 5, 1810)

Perhaps it may not come forth *unseasonably* at this *juncture*, if the distractions occasioned by this *mystery of inequity*, may be thereby so revived in our memories, as to awaken us from that supine security, which again too generally prevails, and put us upon our guard, lest the enemy should be yet within our doors.

—Daniel Horsmanden, original preface,
The New York Conspiracy

PROLOGUE: COLONY OF
NEW YORK, 1712

B EWARE THE AFRICANS, Koromantines and Paw-
paws of the Akan-Asante, kidnapped from West African
shores and brought to the ocean's other side. Warriors, with
anger and reason and nothing to lose, trained in the art of
guerrilla tactics as part of their rites of manhood. Fear them,
Caucasians of the colonies, for they are men born into humanity, raised to be the inheritors of society and not the
beasts of it. They will lead and the rest of the slaves will follow, those other wretches whose own belief in their equality
was a rumor oft denied. Beware, colonists, for now it is your
dying time. It had been two years since the stolen members of
their tribe had been transported to this cold, forest island.
How long had they cached their stolen weapons in the woods
north of the village for this moment? How many outrages
against their humanity had they endured solely because they
knew this time of retribution would come?

The rebel party was formed, ready to pour blood on the
grass of Manhattan isle. Two were women—one joining her

husband, the other pregnant. Two were "Spanish Negroes," kidnapped off conquered Spanish vessels and enslaved on the basis that they were brown, and you could do brown people like that, and there was good money in it. Tonight though, the brown ones would get to pay back the debt. Fully committed, they now moved as one, their loyalty sworn by oath. Pledges insured by the literal collateral of their eternal souls.

You get pain, you get so much pain, that there comes a time that you have to give it back again. Succored by anticipated revenge, the chance to inflict blows in retaliation to those so casually given them. They had waited and now their time had come—two hours past midnight, early one April morning in the year 1712.

April in New York is a curious time. Winter, it gets so damn cold, the polar wind tunneling down the Hudson, that by the end you start to look at the brown naked trees and start to believe that they've got no green in them. You give up on life, because, as March comes to a close, it's already become a thing of faith. Then April and the little buds start popping and you don't just remember life, you believe in it. April in New York is the time of nature's revolution, where, after six months of frigid death, the first daffodils finally scout the invasion of fauna.

The Africans knew to listen to the Earth, not dominate it. Shake off your freeze and come alive. April meant the promise of warm months stretching beyond. A body could make good tracks in the time before October's winds shut things down once more. Walk far enough north, run fast enough, and there was free country up there. Free living.

Later, when it was time to point fingers, the Caucasians said it was the pubs, wasn't it? Those black bastards, you get them drinking, they lose their bloody minds. And maybe the smell of alcohol was among them, spirits swallowed and spilled in tribute for the deed to go down. Maybe the Europeans just needed the rumors of drink to dismiss the event as a drunken moment of rage, an anomaly for an otherwise docile breed of man. Peter the Doctor didn't need to swill Geneva to find his gumption, no indeed. Peter was a free man, he'd tell you, the one free black among them, a man of knowledge, wise in the ways of the old land. Come before him, this man of wisdom. Let him shake the powder on your head that will protect you from the powder that fuels the colonists' guns. Believe in this magic, for it is your belief that gives it strength, which can push you on. His scarred hand reaching into his pouch with cautious solemnity, the Doctor drew forth a magic powder made by the rites of old and anointed all who gathered. Feel its power, feel your own, let the dust of the gods rain down. Become invulnerable to the attack you will surely provoke, children of Africa. Let it cover your clothes as you pray to gods forbidden by name in this heathen land. Consider yourselves prepared for what would follow.

Once I was talking to this G.E.D. class in the Bronx, talking about gentrification and urban renewal and class migration, and this kid asked me, "If you was sent back in time, and was a slave, would you kill yourself?" It had absolutely nothing to do with the topic at hand and its odd posing hinted at why this dude was getting his G.E.D.

in the first place, but I tried to answer him. "No, I probably would not," I told him, citing my family responsibilities as reason: I got kids, a wife, parents. Apparently, this was the wrong answer. He would throw himself off a building, he insisted. I tried to tell him the buildings weren't that tall back then, only two stories, so he'd probably only break his leg, but this knucklehead wasn't trying to listen.

In the darkness, the Africans gathered behind the home of Peter Vantilborough; two of the men who were enslaved by Vantilborough were eager members of the party. As the duo approached the outhouse in order to set it ablaze, the others hid behind the trees and waited, listened to their own nervous panting as they prepared to kill every pink-skinned rescuer who came running. "Light the fire!" came nervous, fast whispers as the Africans crouched around them, feeling most alive in the moment that life was most at risk. Make the deed done, seal the fate tonight. In the back of the yard by the outhouse, kindling in hand, Vantilborough's slaves accomplished their ignition. Sparked the fuse that would change the lives of all who waited eagerly in the shadows beyond.

A will for havoc united the Africans, regardless of ethnicity or birth land. A determination to end the atrocity of their bondage. Soon moonlight was eclipsed as flames copulated around them, flames reveling in greed and consumption, the fire's flicker giving the illusion of motion to the frozen Africans nestled in hiding places all around, muskets, machetes, and swords in hand.

New York was a city of solid brick houses, but the houses

were covered by wooden roofs, and usually wooden store-houses and stables stood right behind them, all packed tightly together like matches in a box. Fire and fear were synonymous. It was great poetry that the key to the community's destruction could be obtained by even its most downtrodden, penniless citizen. In fire was equality. Few men had the ability to build something in this world, but all had the power to destroy in it. Properly placed, one smoldering coal could reduce a rich man to a pauper, turn a controlled community into a chaotic one. When a fire started, only the hurried summoning of the four-year-old fire brigade and the quick formation of a bucket brigade—a line of neighbors passing water from a well or river to the inferno—could offer defense from it. How it shined in the black balls of the Africans' eyes, jumping red and orange that symbolized the return of freedom and all of its meaning which had been denied. Revenge and rage crackled before them, the fire's heat their own, its will for destruction just a sample of what beat in their breasts this night.

The Caucasians came running, you could see their pale, fishlike skin glowing in the night, sense the confusion in their rushed gaits as they jogged forth, still gathering their clothes around them. Wait till they get closer, wait till they get closer, then pull the trigger.

For the first wave of arrivals, their clothes did little to protect them as musket balls ripped through their European garments before they had any understanding of what they'd run into. Five pink men lay dead at the rebels' feet in a dozen seconds, six more ran wounded from the offering. If the gunpowder didn't warn the rest of the city, the wounded would, and the rebels stuffed their muskets with all the speed they could manage, packing in the powder, dropping in the ball. Prepare to shoot, pick them off as they come in.

The colonists quickly raised a militia. They had the numbers, ten to one. They had the arms as well. The Africans knew this would happen. They kept packing their muskets, shooting. Four more pale lives were claimed by the rebels, cut down like ripe cane. Every time another European life was extinguished, the Africans realized a moment of freedom. Rejoice in blood, if nothing else is offered.

It was minutes before the two dozen Africans were overtaken, sent running toward whatever future was left for them. Years of pining, months of planning and hoarding, and in a few minutes off the hour it was done. The Doctor's powder had reminded them that they were brave, done little more, yet all that was expected of it. The lucky ones had already been slain for their efforts, been given the release of warriors. For the rest, it was time to retreat from the immediate reality. On an island, into a foreign land, in cold climate alien to them. Not running to anything—just running.

Shocked in the middle of the night, their own dark, guilt-ridden fears given form and force before them, the Caucasians thought their Judgment Day was upon them. A hasty dispatch was sent to the British troops at the garrison, miles below at the southern tip of Manhattan Island. But before the British soldiers could even arrive, the Africans had disappeared into darkness. Regrouping possibly, ending the first wave in the larger war.

As colonists rushed through the night trying to unite against the opposition, fear and confusion reigned. Among the predominantly English and Dutch colonists a call to arms went out, demanding an end to any infectious thoughts of mass African uprising. The rebels kept running, the calls to arms echoing behind them. The sounds of the dogs barking their own excitement at the growing hunt.

North, go north, just run. Away from the mob the whites have created to own your bodies once more. Run back into the darkness as your own attempt at light is being doused behind you. Don't look back, there's nothing behind you anymore.

Not that there was far to go. Manhattan, the island, inescapably finite. They wouldn't make it far enough north that crossing the narrows of the Harlem River into the mainland Bronx beyond would even become an issue. The militia, without need to hide by day nor avoid the main trails, made it to the top of the island past Inwood before the Africans could ever hope to manage to. Even if the Africans had broken through that tightly sealed barrier, further reinforcements from Long Island and Westchester quickly swarmed in as second and third armies. The Africans were stuck in the woods, hiding. Many of them were new arrivals; some had been on the island less than two years, the others only months and could not even speak English. Few would have even seen snow before arrival and lacked any practical knowledge of how to survive in the harsh North American winter. The pain of April is the summer heat is forgotten at sun's setting, the night is as cold as a day from three months before. Yet still, stride and stumble, they moved. Callused feet numb and blistered, flesh scraped raw by the branches of the wild brush they hid among. Too scared to stick to any path recognized, listening between the rhythm of their own footfalls to hear of other beats of feet behind them.

Sometimes, when in Central Park, I can hear them coming, still. Close your eyes, think, and it's there. Like hell's still behind them. Fleeing steadily, birds from a storm. Stand in the right place in Central Park and you can look up and only foliage and bedrock will fill your vision and the specter of the lost Manhattan is revealed. The true New York, a place beyond skyscrapers and concrete, out of time and beyond the industrial imagination. Then, you can almost see them there, past the tree line, hiding. Standing as still as they can and praying to those failed gods to elude your focus. Wasting among the shrubbery. Waiting for you to pass so they can breathe once more.

Stuck without shelter or food in New York's cold April nights, facing certain death regardless of course of action, the six ex-slaves responsible for organizing the rebellion exerted a final act of defiance, one last moment of leadership. Weapons turned against themselves, those six chose to take their own lives before the slavers could get the chance. Ending the pain of starvation, fear, and exposure in an act of small victory.

. The rest of the Africans were much less fortunate.

There was no quiet end to this engagement, even for those

who admitted defeat. Near collapse, the surviving rebels turned themselves in to the colonists, only to be thrown in with all the other slaves that had been rounded up in the mass hysteria they'd help create. In response to a conspiracy of two dozen, seventy slaves were seized and thrown into jail by the panicking pink skins. No brown New Yorker, regardless of innocence or alibi, was safe from a population of colonists who had seen their dominance challenged, their sense of security revealed as illusion. It was madness, and even some of those in the moment could see its true nature. Covering the event, the *Boston News Letter* compared the shrill reactionary insanity that now infected the New York colony to the curious incident that had recently taken place in the northern colony of Massachusetts, in that town of Salem. People were suspicious of everything. Damn, even the shadows, for they are black, too.

Courtly justice was quick; the village needed a reason to calm once more. Out of the twenty-seven black people brought to trial, twenty-one were found guilty and sentenced to death. The six others owed their freedom to a lack of incriminating evidence and the intervention of the colony's governor, whose physical distance from the city also provided him a sense of reason currently scarce on the isle. Solemnly, New York slowly began returning to normal. As a true sign of peace, politics took dominance once more. Serious rebellion cases before the court rapidly devolved into petty sabotage. During their trials, the Africans' welfare was often decided not on personal guilt but on the political party affiliation of the man who enslaved them. African lives, which for a moment, had been taken very seriously, were once again treated as utterly trivial, now that the element of fear was again removed.

Those that were chosen to die did so openly, cruelly, creatively. A public burning was always a crowd-pleaser. The victim was brought from the jail in chains, tied to a stake above a large pile of dry wood as the crowd jeered and threw rotten vegetables or whatever else was close to hand. It was an occasion as joyous as morbid, a festive frenzy to base one's day around. A cheap day on the town, perfect to bring your whole family. First came the smoke, the victim struggling to breathe a line of clear air. Then the flames lifting up began to overwhelm them, heating their irons so that they were sautéed in their own chains. As to dogs before dinner, the smell of cooked meat further enticed the crowd.

If burning wasn't your thing, the city had other offerings. Less fortunate Africans were tied to a rack for a longer-lasting show, hands shackled above, feet below, their bodies stretched slowly until arms were pulled from their sockets, human legs pulled from their hips like one would a drumstick from a chicken. Those screams, now that was entertainment. Will they first faint or bleed to death, or simply die from the excitement of it all? It was hard to say, you just had to stay for the whole show. Make a little side bet on it, if you were the sort to wager.

Now, the fortunate Africans were gibbeted: hanged by the noose, to speed things along. A little death jig, suspended on the end of the rope, a broken neck, and you were done. Now that was the way to go. Mind you, the contents of your bowels now belonged to your bloomers, but it wasn't like you could smell it anymore. In mere minutes death could be yours. A merciful alternative provided by an enlightened society. Every splash of blood was a sign of order returned. Every scream of agony a declaration that what once was normal would pass for such again. The crowds roared, compensated for their fear with entertainment.

Behind the symbolic action of public execution, the judicial laws backed up this resolve practically. Slaves could now be punished by their captors without impediment, no beating too severe, no crime too small. No more than three slaves could legally gather without the presence of a white to oversee them. No black was allowed outside after nightfall without a lantern to clearly illuminate him. Any slave found in possession of a firearm would exchange it for several lashings. The few Africans that lived free on the island were no longer permitted to own land or a house upon it. Those slave owners who would see fit to free their human property would find themselves practically barred by the near impossible tax of two hundred pounds if they did so: four to six times the price of buying a slave outright, ten times the average yearly salary, a small fortune that hindered even the most generous intentions. So thorough were the Europeans in their plan of oppression, they even denied access to their own white god, going as far as prosecuting one of their own who dared to teach His name to the blackened race.

What very few rights the African captives maintained were summarily stripped, all hope for freedom dismantled. Those who had little now had much less than that, becoming a people without control of their owned bodies or the spirits they housed. The only say in their destiny being the greatest one—to choose to live the half-life prescribed to them or to choose not to live at all. The white colonist reacted not by simply squashing a rebellion, but by crushing the very people it represented. The blacks now had nothing. And what could be feared from just a memory of defiance?

To call the Slave Revolt of 1712 a failure is to assume that these enslaved ever had a chance at success. Nothing could come of it, other than the act itself.

But the act was important. The act was worth enough.

So at that G.E.D. class, this knucklehead says he'd just kill himself with a sword or something, maybe take a few crackers with him first, but then he'd end it.

"No, you wouldn't," I dismissed him. This cat, he didn't like that, he didn't like being dismissed. He said, "You don't know me, you don't know what I'm capable of."

This was true, I acknowledged, but I told him I did know this: you are the descendant of the slaves that didn't choose to end their lives. You are the descendant of the slaves that chose to keep their heads down, swallow their pride, and wait till the time was right. Even if it took centuries. You are the descendant of the slaves that chose to live.

But the stories in this book, these are tales of those other enslaved Africans. The martyrs among the millions of human lives destroyed by the European slave trade. The ones that chose meaningful death over the chattel life.

LOOSE CHANGE

SILVER HAS ALWAYS MADE GOOD stealing. You can hammer the metal down if you put your muscle to it, or melt it if you got the know-how. No matter what you do, it's still worth something. You take a silver spoon, right—it's worth the same even after it's been slipped up your sleeve, smuggled to a local blacksmith, and reverted once more to its liquid form. Best part, no one can lay claim to it afterward, prove you've been stealing. That's good investment, that is. Or, if you're lucky enough to get your callused mitts on actually silver coins, all the better, am I right? Instantly, you become a citizen of leisure. Mind you, this is the reason that it's important for those who already own silver to guard their own. For those with coins in their possession, that goes even more so.

Mrs. Hogg was a smart lady. A businesswoman, she knew to look after her own. Counting up Spanish coins as she worked the counter at her husband's general store that Saturday in late February 1741, it must have been with this particular weight in mind. Spanish coins: proof the Spanish were good for something. The English, they'd no desire to see their own currency drained across the globe, so their thirteen American colonies chose the silver coins of the Spaniards instead. Even with the two nations at war, this currency remained. Silver, hard tender, a one-pound coin being nearly as much as a seaman might make in a month. Focused on the import of the accounting at hand, making sure every last cent was duly noted, the weight of the monetary task must have pulled Mrs. Hogg's focus away from her physical surroundings. Still, it was that primal sense that told her there were eyes upon her. Someone is watching, Mrs. Hogg. There is more to this world than the money in your hand, Mrs. Hogg—there are also the people who *want* the money in your hand. Looking up from her accounting, Mrs. Hogg shot a glance across the store to see one of the patrons, a young soldier, Wilson of the Famborough man-of-war, staring directly back at her. Or more specifically, staring directly at the contents of her purse.

It was not fair to come to immediate judgments about soldiers. After all, were these not the men of England, their defenders in this savage new world? Somebody's got to be a soldier, who else would protect the citizenry from all the other soldiers? If not for these warriors, there would be no one to guard the colony against the whims of the red heathens, or more important, against those Spanish conquerors for the pope, the Papist enemies of freedom. Besides, Wilson was only a seventeen-year-old infantryman who'd made a friendly habit of stopping by the store to socialize with its employees. A harmless little bloke, weighing less wet than one of Mrs. Hogg's ample thighs. Still, there was a general morale of contempt among the troops who loosely protected the New York colony. Not exactly England's finest; they could be seen stumbling away from the island's many public houses more often than standing ground at their fort. Let's be honest—with all the good money to be made in business in this new land, usually the type of men who walked with the infantry were those who had no other path to follow.

So Wilson was looking. So what, Mrs. Hogg shrugged it off, thinking no more on the matter. Can't get bothered by every little thing. In fact, Mrs. Hogg left her Spanish coins right there in the store where they had been counted, the moment of discomfort decidedly forgotten, sent to the dull parts of the brain with the rest of the day's rubbish. It wasn't until Mrs. Hogg arrived at the shop the following morning and saw the front door splintered open, found the contents of her beloved store rifled through, goods knocked to the floor, picked apart, and missing, that the lingering gaze of young Wilson returned to her, and those doubts quickly, oh so quickly, came flooding back. Her body moving almost as fast as her mind, she rushed to the counter where she had secured her treasured Spanish silver coins, only to find them vanished as well.

A shrewd woman, a businesswoman, this Mrs. Hogg. Sure, it was her husband's store on paper, but everyone knew who really ran it. She knew how to deal with the matter. After reporting the incident to the constable, cleaning up the mess, and preparing for another day's commerce, Mrs. Hogg played it cool. Spent the day staring up at the door every time the bell went off with a patron's entry. Waited patiently the rest of that Saturday until she was rewarded, and young Wilson sauntered in as he made his social rounds. What else could he do but play this day like every other day, as if innocence was never even a question.

Mrs. Hogg watched the door close behind Wilson, let him enter all the way into the shop before cornering him.

"Come on, boy. You saw me counting those coins, didn't you? Don't answer, I know you did. I saw you," she told him. "Only you saw where I placed them."

Despite Wilson's obvious guilt, Mrs. Hogg's tone was almost diplomatic. She needed something from him, and made clear that as long as he played along, her tone would not change timbre.

"Maybe . . . maybe you might have told one of your mates, am I right? One of your fellow soldiers about what you saw? There's room for absolution, boy. Nobody's saying you did anything yourself, but perhaps you might have been a little loose with your words. Taken advantage of, as it were. Maybe, Mr. Wilson, you might know a bit more about the crime that was committed right here where you're standing?" Mrs. Hogg hid the implied accusation and threat politely behind the question marks, where they wouldn't get in the way of the information needed.

"I did happen to see one John Gwin spending silver loosely, giving out cash to a slave named Cuffee at the Hughsons' public house," young Wilson offered nervously, his own culpability hidden behind the shroud of coincidence. Looking around as he confessed to see who was witnessing his betrayal.

John Hughson could have avoided disaster and history if he'd just kept his pudgy white arse in Yonkers, tilled the land in quiet obscurity, and enjoyed the tranquility that life had to offer (of course, our John was never much for peace and quiet). No, instead of playing it safe, John fell in love with a woman who wanted more, and he decided to want more with her. To come down to the city and have a go at fulfilling their hunger. Those first days down the Hudson started out honest enough, at first. Johnnie-boy was making his wages as a leather worker then, an honest trade if not particularly exciting. But the honest, simple life never really managed to pay the Hughsons' bills, did it? And really, in these days of endless opportunity of this great new land, what was the sense in not trying to grab a bit of the fortune it had to offer? This little settlement on the Hudson, it had real potential. Hughson, he saw that. Just wanted to get in on a bit of the action, really.

So Sarah and John Hughson opened a tavern instead. Two, actually. The first attempt, which thrived for a bit on the east side of the island, quickly died, succumbing to the complaints of neighbors that it served the worst sort of clientele. The second, on the west side, not far from the Trinity churchyard and the African burial grounds, proved more stable. There was always money to be made in spirits, on this thirsty island— whether dealing firkins of drink directly to the natives who came south to trade otter or beaver skins for rum, or setting up your own public house. The drink business was one you could count on. With the colony now a century old, and the population passing fifty thousand—sixty if you counted the Africans—fresh water was hard to come by within the limits of the city. It was always a safer bet (and a more enjoyable one) to take your drink distilled. At least to add to the water for taste, or to kill the bloody smell of that well sludge you got in town. Without a nice pint of hard cider in the cold months, many a lad would lack completely any nutritious fruit for his diet. They were long months before the meadows came alive in green again and you could grab a real apple in your hand. And regardless, even without issues of health taken into consideration, New Yorkers just liked a cup. New York drank more annually than even those in the bigger cities, north and south, Boston and Philadelphia. A taste left over from the days of New Amsterdam, perhaps, from decades before when the Dutch ruled. Back then, desperate to get any white people to populate this savage land, the colony was filled with a . . . a lower sort. Those that no other outpost would have accepted. Got so bad back then, the great Peter Stuyvesant himself tried to close the public houses at a mere nine o'clock, and keep the lower-class indentured workers out of the pubs altogether. But that was the Dutch, a more permissive sort. Not that the English could really talk; their colonies were now going through 7,750,000 gallons of whiskey a year, so there were very few sober fingers to do any pointing.

Honestly, no law or any of the other measures could get people to stop gathering at pubs for a drink and a laugh. Market rule: As long as people want a product, someone will be willing to sell it to them. Still, the Hughsons faced all the normal difficulties of starting a small business; the competition for those thirsty patrons was fierce and countless. If the other drinking establishments were going to stay open past curfew, how could one humble owner close early and still stay in the black? So what if the Hughsons broke the law by selling to the Africans as well as to the Europeans? It is a rich man who would walk away from a coin just because he didn't like the color of the hand it dropped from. Yes, it was against the law to serve a slave, or for slaves even to congregate in a white establishment, but it could be argued (and was) that the more the Negroes drank in their idle time, the less likely they were to do anything dangerous. And if, on occasion, some of these dark men happened to obtain a few loose items of their master's property to pay for their tab, who can blame a struggling businessman for brokering a transaction that would have taken place regardless? Common Council law had been forbidding whites to entertain blacks in their homes, sell them liquor, or take goods, or money, from them since the 1712 incident, but really, the more restrictive the laws, the less people followed them. One couldn't always make a living just pouring Geneva and hosting cockfights. So the Hughsons did a bit of discreet matchmaking as well, between potential buyer and motivated sellers, taking a bit of tribute off the top to make ends meet. "Diversification" was the business term for it.

★   ★   ★

Young Wilson was in a spot of trouble. The constables surrounded him, and even more threatening was Mrs. Hogg herself, the wronged party, pushing him on. "Tell them! Come on, boy," Mrs. Hogg insisted. "Tell them what you told me."

"Well, right, I did happen to notice the mistress here with her coins, just admiring them. And, well, a few drams later at Hughson's pub and, well—"

"Come on!" Mrs. Hogg slapped the back of the boy's head. With the force of the blow, the rest of the confession seemed to pop right out of him.

"The bloke I was talking about it to, word is today that he's just come into some money, too. It was the one John Gwin," Wilson blurted. "The one what's a customer at Hughson's regular-like. In fact, he's there now. Mind you, if he asks who told you . . ."

John Gwin? The name meant nothing to the constables, but the mention of Hughson's pub was enough to arouse suspicion on its own. It was known to be one of the darkest of the many nuisance public houses across the city, where the laws of the municipality were routinely flouted. Where blacks and the lowest sort of whites came to get drunk on spirits and grumble and curse the gentle citizens who stood above them. Only a few months before, the tavern had been raided, and John Hughson found guilty of serving slaves. The only reason the fat bastard had been spared was that he was a first offender. So much for mercy. In the time since, Hughson's reputation for disrepute had only grown stronger, and the constables were just waiting for the opportunity to catch him committing the crimes of which they suspected him. "Suspected" is probably too light a verb, even. The scamp fenced so many stolen goods that the slaves had nicknamed his tavern "Oswego," in honor of that great trading hub to the north.

Hughson's door was thrown open, and the constables poured in, in full fury, ready to seize all present. Not much of a task, it turned out: Hughson's was vacant, chairs unoccupied, not a cup filled in the tavern, just the smell of stale drink and tobacco. There was not a man in sight, and surely no soldier named Gwin. Only one lone Negro stood in the hall, a man in his twenties leaning quietly against the chimney, casually smoking his pipe as he watched them until they left again. Negroes, of course, were not English soldiers, not even real men at all, so the man was paid as much attention to as the candles on the walls. Disappointed at their foray for justice being averted, the officers moped back out and turned their frustration back on the one captive they did have in hand, young Wilson.

"'Fess up, boy! You did the robbery yourself, didn't you? We've checked Hughson's, and there's no soldier name Gwin hanging about there."

"But I—wait, you say soldier? No, no, that's the problem. John Gwin the slave, sirs. You know, smokes a pipe, green coat."

Hurrying back, much to their surprise and relief, the brazen scoundrel was still there, his position unchanged. "Back so soon?" he had the nerve to ask with a smile. Presenting a calm pose before being thrown into irons.

★ ★ ★

"John Gwin" was how he was known to young Wilson, but he was "Caesar" to most else, a ranking officer in the Geneva Club, called as such by all those who would indulge the proper title and Masonic manners he and his African mates had appropriated. And once identified, this slave's dark history would become appropriated as well.

The Geneva Club was formed, or more accurately named, after Caesar and his group had been caught robbing barrels of Geneva (the Dutch gin so popular in the city) from a local inn. Despite the severity of this crime, Caesar, as well as his running partner, a fellow named Prince, had escaped the hangman's noose—as was often prescribed for such a transgression—and instead bore the incalculable pain of a good sound flogging instead. It was a wretched thing to be owned, but if you were it was a good thing to be enslaved by men too busy with their own lives to be overly concerned with the off-hours in yours. And powerful enough to keep their property (you) from being destroyed (killed) for its (your) transgressions (petty larceny, theft, burglary, distribution of stolen goods, etc.).

Now, looking for evidence in this new caper, the city constables immediately set about searching Hughson's for the stolen silver coins and the speckled linen that had also gone missing from Mrs. Hogg's store. The lucre had to be in there, somewhere. Where else could it be? There hadn't been enough time to go hide it in the woods. And, as such, they wasted the entire day searching, garnering nothing but mounting frustration and doubts for their trouble. Regardless, Caesar was held in custody, if for no crime other than being black and supremely arrogant.

The seasoned criminal that he was, Caesar sat in jail with some measure of confidence. They had nothing on him. The boy, Wilson? He was a joke, everyone knew that. Without a confession the authorities could do nothing, and Caesar, in his cell, had no intention of making one available to them. No, they'd need more evidence than the guilty whimpers of some snot-nosed soldier whose own innocence was suspect. The guilty are always calm upon arrest. It's the innocent ones who do the most sweating. In his cell Caesar was just—to use a term his co-ethnicists would come to employ centuries later— *chilling*.

Rather than wasting their time with a suspect who had no intention of offering further assistance, the constables decided to call in the rest of the players so that the drama could properly unfold. Gather those two other known members of the Geneva Club, Cuffee and Prince, and bring them in. Wrest them from their masters' houses. Even better, let's go back to the source, try our luck on someone with really something to lose.

The following day, John Hughson and his wife, Sarah, were yanked from their home and strong-armed down to the jail. The tavern was searched once more by Mr. Mills, the under-sheriff, and the other constables, just as it had been the day before, as it would be the day after, with identical results. They found nothing.

Surrounded by his accusers, John Hughson feigned more innocence than he was born with.

"No, no, you got the wrong man," he insisted. "There seems to be some sort of mistake here. I am but a simple tavern keeper. A man of limited means and ambitions. How about I offer you gentlemen a round after all this is over, what say you? It is no matter."

Impressively, Hughson was consistent in his denials, no matter how much his interrogators drilled him. No matter how many times they looked at his tongue and knew, by instinct, that those were lies flying off it. Frustrated, thwarted, the constables had no choice but to let John and Sarah Hughson free once more, to watch them walk off into the darkness.

Walking home in the cold March night, John Hughson breathed a bit of relief.

"I don't know what you're so bloody happy about," Sarah chided him, humiliated, and still trembling. "We almost lost our heads in there. We're lucky to be free, you daft muggins. This could be the end of it all."

"Oh hush, my love. They got nothing," John insisted. "Nothing," pulling her hand to his. "That was the worst of it, they threw all they could and nothing stuck. Trust me, dear, our troubles are behind us."

It was with growing comfort that John and Sarah returned to their inn that night, closing the door behind them. After a long two days, they were finally home, safe inside. Completely unaware that their impending ruin would come not from outside their household, but from the weakest voice within.

NOT CUTE ENOUGH

To be poor in England in the eighteenth century was not simply a shame, it was a crime. English poor laws had been in effect since the fourteenth century, but while far from a new phenomenon, poverty had a special meaning as the empire became global. Before expansion into the new lands, the dirty and impoverished were something that the English elite simply had to endure. No matter how harsh the penalties for poverty and indolence, no matter how many perished from starvation or disease, there were always more to replace the unwashed masses. Now, with the discovered countries, England could unburden itself of its human refuse, recycling its undesirables as fodder for the construction of the empire. In America, in exchange for years of free labor, the cost of relocating the poor, the convicted, the indigent was covered by the landowner who would make use of them. At the end of their service, the indentured servant would at least have the chance to start a new life in the land of opportunity, usually with some sort of severance to usher him or her along. Often indentured servants finished their terms with a trade learned or parcel of land gained, the fruit of their time in captivity.

Unlike in the Chesapeake colonies or those English outposts to the north, the New York colony had few indentured servants, and those they did attract were seldom "transports," or convicts, but "freewillers," free immigrants who chose on their own to enter a period of bond. That there was such a difference in culture between colonies of the same flag can be attributed to the fact that the city of New York, whether under Dutch, English, or later American control, has always been about money, as opposed to religious freedom or creating a utopia. New York means business, *is* business. This alone informs every aspect of New York's character, from conception forward.

Slavery was about business. As far as economic value to the employer, slavery just couldn't be beat. It was a steal—literally. For the slaveholders, it was impossible to get a better deal than the one-time payment slavery demanded. For the immigrating European working class, slavery was impossible to compete against. Unlike in the other regions where slaves were largely utilized for unskilled, manual labor, the slaves of Manhattan Island were often skilled artisans, trained in the crafts and trades of their masters, or retained specifically for their skill to serve as craftsmen for households. By training slaves for such specified labor, slaveholders could also hire out their captives for additional profits when demand arose—something particularly convenient in what was largely a port town, with ships arriving regularly in need of various forms of labor. Slavery also (and this was no small thing) alleviated the constant risk of having former apprentices leave to branch out on their own, going from an artisan's much needed assistant to his much unwanted competitor. Because of this, tensions between poor workers struggling to make a living and wageless slaves would begin early in New York, and find several eruption points along the line long before the hideous Draft Riots of the Civil War would spark one of the city's greatest atrocities.

In New York, apprenticeship among whites was a willfully neglected practice. In 1737, lieutenant governor George Clarke warned that "the artificers complain and with too much reason of the pernicious custom of breeding slaves to trades whereby the honest and industrious tradesmen are reduced to poverty for want of employ, and many of them forced to leave us to seek their living in other countries." White flight, the old-fashioned way. In an attempt to make indentured servitude more attractive to employers, in 1711 the term of indentured service was lengthened from four to eleven years. This helped a bit, but with only 203 apprentices indentured in the colony between 1718 and 1727, it in no way took care of the massive demand of an expanding city. In 1734, colonial governor William Cosby echoed the fears of white Manhattan when he said, "I see with concern that whilst the neighboring Provinces are filled with honest, useful and labourious [sic] white people, the truest riches and surest strength of country, this Province seems regardless of . . . the disadvantages that attend the too great importation of negroes and convicts."

Without enough white workers to go around, New York

became a city that was carried by black, skilled hands. Still, there were some advantages for adventurous Brits to become indentured servants here. As one of the few and prized, for instance, you were likely to encounter better treatment and status than in colonies overrun with the indentured. And of course, damn near anything was an improvement over the chances for the lower class in overcrowded, class-obsessed England.

Perhaps this is what motivated young Mary Burton to choose to lease herself to John Hughson as a house servant, as opposed to any of the other options available to her. Perhaps, as it was later insinuated (by a less than objective party), it was that Mary had arrived at the Hughsons' as damaged goods after she'd left the house of her last employ pregnant with the master's child. Inflammatory, certainly speculative accusations— Mary Burton was only sixteen years old. Still, how else would a young girl end up in servitude to such a disreputable house such as the Hughsons', unless it was that she had nowhere else to go? Much was said of Mary Burton. Most deserved. Very little complimentary.

Who would think that such a humble girl could do so much damage, could, in just a few months, cause the deaths of scores and the terror of thousands? The following day after the under-sheriff, Mills, and his constables had searched Hughson's home a final time, Mary Burton entered the house of a neighbor, James Kannady, one of the constables whom Mary had just witnessed doing the searching. Mary came under the guise of borrowing a pound of candles, but it was just an excuse to get in the door and hear the latest gossip on the Hogg burglary. If Sarah Hughson had known her little disobedient, loose-lipped servant girl had snuck off to Kannady's she would have surely taken the switch to her, but it was worth it.

Mary didn't even have to broach the subject; Mrs. Kannady seized the opportunity.

"Listen, girl," Mrs. Kannady prodded her young neighbor. "If you know anything, you'd do best to discover it now, lest you yourself should be brought into trouble."

"Madam, I . . . I can't," Mary dodged coyly. "Begging your pardon, it's not my place to say."

"Love, you're forced to work in that house of sin but no one begrudges you for it. You're young, you don't want to spoil your life over that lot. If you know anything, you tell me, and my husband will see to it that you're freed from your master."

Mary Burton pulled away from Mrs. Kannady, candles in hand. The thoughts of freedom were intoxicating, the temptation overwhelming. The only problem: She actually had no information to offer.

Still that did not stop her. "I've things to say, madam," Mary told her, "but my mistress will be waiting. Tomorrow, though, I will come with news for you."

"By the morrow my husband will have already found the stolen goods by himself," Mrs. Kannady pushed. "Now is your chance, girl," she persisted, sensing that Mary Burton was ever eager to say more.

However, Mary just shrugged and giggled her response back at her. "He's not cute enough," she said in a near whisper, "for he has already trod upon them."

Not cute enough? Not sufficiently shrewd? The words haunted Mrs. Kannady long after Mary Burton had left her door. That night, when her husband came home from work, Mrs. Kannady retold her story with passion and insistence, inspiring the off-duty officer to tackle the issue at hand that very evening. Gathering together in a small posse consisting of the Kannadys, Under-Sheriff Mills and his wife, the victimized shop owners Mr. and Mrs. Hogg, as well as several more constables, they stormed the Hughsons' tavern in search of answers.

This search was an act of dedication, not simply an act of service. Both sheriffs and constables worked in their roles only part-time. They were less keepers of the peace than citizen officers of the court. Colonial New York's sheriff functioned primarily as a representative of the judicial system, relegated to retrieving the accused in order to be brought before the bar. The constables were appointed by the court on a yearly basis, again, worked only part-time, and were paid per assignment. While it might be thought that the Kannadys were ever eager because of the commission they would receive, the salary was paltry, little more than a token. Few constables stayed on after their year's appointment. The job paid next to nothing, and, invariably, put them at odds with their neighbors.

These were jobs done strictly out of civic duty.

At the tavern front, it was Mrs. Mills's wish that she and her husband go in first and retrieve young Mary Burton from this den of iniquity. Once out on the road, Mrs. Kannady could then continue interrogation of the girl.

So the Mills went in with that simple plan. The door closed

behind them, and then . . . nothing. The others waited behind them, staring at the door, their apprehension peaking as the moments ticked. "Any minute now" never came, and, patience and decorum abandoning her, Mrs. Kannady gave up, and stormed the tavern. As the door swung open, to her surprise she saw Mr. and Mrs. Mills were just sitting there in the parlor as Mary Burton, standing in front of them, offered up her complete innocence.

"I don't know what she's talking about. I never said no such thing," Mary was protesting. "The Hughsons are decent people, wrongly persecuted. They had nothing to do with—"

"Stop the lies!" Mrs. Kannady interrupted, walking straight up to the girl and grabbing her by the wrists.

For a few moments, in the face of confusion, Mary Burton considered she might slough off her earlier indiscretion as nothing more than a misunderstanding, delusion, even a lie. With Mrs. Kannady before her, however, whatever illusion Mary held that this older woman would simply let the issue go was abandoned. Hushed, nervous, anxious, the servant girl changed her tactic altogether.

Leaning forward, her eyes full of true fear, Mary whispered, "It was them, not me. The black scoundrels in this wretched place will surely kill me. Have mercy."

Together, the Kannadys and Mills yanked Mary Burton out of the tavern, onto the street, and into the Manhattan evening. Hughson's drinking establishment was situated along the island's southwestern edge, near where the World Trade Center would briefly sit centuries later. With the village transitioning into farmland not far beyond, the pub was close to the edge of town, but it was still a well-populated area with citizens strolling around the streets. Workers, free and enslaved, traveled to and from the neighboring piers where ships were serviced before they sailed up the Hudson or out into the Atlantic bound for distant ports and faraway continents. Once she felt herself securely out of range from any prying eyes that might be watching her from the tavern, with a little prodding, Mary Burton loosened again.

"Now speak, girl," Mrs. Kannady pushed her. "Tell us all that you know and you will still be spared. Is Hughson involved in Hogg's theft?"

Mary didn't respond with words at first. Reaching a hand into her pocket, she pulled out one Spanish silver coin. Cold hard evidence, undeniable.

"Mrs. Hogg," she said, offering up the coin, "I think this belongs to you."

Mrs. Hogg jumped forward, snatching the silver out of the girl's hand. "Where did you get this?" she demanded.

"The Negroes," was Mary's solemn reply.

The group was excited, satisfied—finally, evidence of what they all knew must be true. So aroused were they by this substantiation of their hard felt suspicions, that no one bothered to question *why* Mary might have been given the coin in the first place. They were too busy celebrating their assurance that justice was served to question the motives or reliability of their new witness.

To resolve the situation, Mary Burton was taken to Alderman Bancker, governor of the district, with Mrs. Kannady further declaring in front of the official her promise that the indentured servant, Burton, would be freed from her master in payment for testifying.

"They will murder me," Mary beseeched them. "The Hughsons or the Negroes will surely poison me if I'm discovered," she insisted.

"Nonsense, dear," comforted the alderman. "You will go into Mr. Mills's custody; he shall protect you. As for Hughson, I will have him standing before me within the hour."

For his part, John Hughson had known it was trouble as soon as Mary Burton had been dragged out from his place. "That nasty little wench," he thought to himself as the constables arrived for him. He'd known it was trouble as soon as she was dragged out of the the tavern, no matter how much he had bribed her. Surely it was she, Mary Burton, the little girl with the big mouth, and now he was in bigger trouble.

Unforeseen and to his credit, Alderman Bancker did not presume Hughson's guilt in the matter at all. Bancker studied the tavern owner as he made his protestations of innocence, coming to the conclusion, despite the man's obvious nervousness, that Hughson's denials were truthful in nature.

Still it was surely evident Hughson's tavern was clearly of the lowest, nuisance sort. Rowdy, to say the least. And given this, the alderman said to him, "In light of this evidence, Mr. Hughson, you must assist the constables in their efforts at last and help reveal the stolen goods and those guilty of acquiring them."

"Certainly, sir." Hughson smiled, showing his rough teeth back at the alderman. "Why, they have but to ask and I shall be there, assisting and such. I shall give it my full attention, and prove to you, sir, my innocence in the matter."

See, things weren't so bad, Hughson judged. Just got to give a little. Just got to get to the bottom of this theft (of which he continued to contend he knew nothing) and, by so cooperating, clear his name. A good plan, considering the circumstances, and if played intelligently it could be to his advantage and see him to the end of this fiasco.

Unfortunately, while John Hughson could fairly be called many things, none of them would be "intelligent." Instead of reappearing with some incidental trace evidence that might lead the authorities away from his own culpability, the taverner took it one step further and returned instead with *all* the stolen goods in question, silver coins, speckled linen, everything. The constables looked at the loot in disbelief, then peered back at the beaming Hughson. There he stood, so happy and relieved to have the whole thing up and done with. Completely unconscious of the fact that he'd just given proof that he was in direct possession of the stash the whole time, substantiating definitively his own utter guilt in the matter.

Ah, the genius of John Hughson!

"MARY BURTON, OF THE CITY OF NEW-YORK, SPINSTER"

THERE MAY HAVE BEEN WORSE COLONIES THAN New York in which to find yourself standing accused before the court in the eighteenth century, other places where mere accusation alone seemed to be counted as evidence of wrongdoing. In nearby New Haven, for instance, 90 percent of defendants brought to trial were found guilty. In New York, at least, nearly half of the accused on trial were given the chance to prove their innocence (or feign it). And considering that the Hogg crime involved theft of personal property that amounted to a small fortune, it was somewhat to John Hughson's advantage that the trial was being held on the American continent altogether, for this was a time of even harsher punishment for thievery back in fair England, where intolerance for such sins had resulted in frequent capital sentences. While the hangman's noose was offered for the crime of thievery in the new land as well, that option was rarely selected. Even if convicted, with any luck, Hughson might be sentenced to a good flogging, or at worst a pillorying, both of which it was, theoretically, possible to live through.

Colonial justice was made more complicated for its defendants by its simplicity: The justice of the case served not only as a "judge" in the modern sense, but also played the role of prosecutor. Judges were responsible for choosing to go to trial, gathering the incriminating evidence, securing the prosecuting witnesses, as well as interrogating both them and the suspects. It was an arrangement that made impartiality, at best, difficult; a power dynamic that made any trial without an impartial judge no more than a formality to sentencing. To make matters worse, most judges in the colonies had no qualifications for the job other than that they were wealthy landowners with enough political clout to wrangle these influential, though part-time, appointments. A census taken two decades after the events of 1741 found that only 41 percent of New York's judges had any proper legal training or experience before taking the mantle. As prominent New Yorker, and former legal apprentice, William Livingston would put it in 1745, "There is perhaps no Set of men that bear so ill a Character in the Estimation of the Vulgar, as the Gentlemen of the Long Robe."

Standing before the court to hear the charges, John Hughson was joined by his wife, Sarah, per the court's order, along with their lodger, Margaret Sorubiero.

Margaret Sorubiero, also known as Margaret Salingburgh, was better known as Peggy Kerry. What could be said of a common Irish woman who lived above this tavern known to be populated by lowly whites and Negroes? That she was a prostitute, of course; it was unproven but there was no need (there were hundreds of such women in the area around the fort). That her board and lodging were paid for by Caesar, the primary Negro in question, was proof enough. The reason for this latest addition to the alderman's request list was made clear when the Hughsons and Peggy laid eyes on the court's first witness.

"Mary Burton, of the city of New York, spinster, aged about sixteen years, being sworn, deposed," the clerk called, and the slight peasant girl took center stage in the drama. Avoiding the penetrating glances of her former housemates, Mary nervously began:

"Must have been two o'clock in the morning I'd seen him, that Negro, Caesar, the one what also goes by the name John Gwin (or is it Quin?), sneaking in through the window of Miss Peggy. Yes, Peggy Kerry, this white woman. The Negro slipped right into her bedroom window in the dark of night, he did. What's more, he often made her bed his own, made a habit of it. God's truth."

The stage-whispered curses of the accused beside her threatened to cut Mary Burton's narrative short, but the mortified gasps from the rest of the room pushed her on, fed her with attention, giving her the strength to continue.

"The following morn, the speckled linen, it was right there," Mary went on. "I seen the stolen fabric," she told them, but what went unsaid was that Caesar had seen Mary see it, her eyes grow wide at the sight of the fine cloth. Mary failed to mention that Caesar had thrown her two pieces of silver to shut her up, or that Peggy cut an apron from the material to give to her to ensure her silence. Mary was not on trial here. She was simply an innocent corrupted.

So much money in his hand as Caesar sat that morning in the tavern, gloating. So much more than he could have ever earned honestly, far more intoxicating to him than any liquor he could buy. Mary couldn't tell them that, because she couldn't imagine the feeling, but she could tell other things.

"Caesar was all casual-like, too, the cat with a mouse, he was. Bought a pair of proper white stockings for his Peggy right then from my master, added two mugs of punch on top to get his silver's worth. The master and the mistress both seen the speckled linen that morning as well, as sure as I did."

As Mary spoke, the Hughsons sat in terror and disbelief. As they listened they blustered with indignation at such betrayal from this hypocritical and scandalous girl!

"After Under-Sheriff Mills done arrived the first time in search of this soldier, Gwin, Mrs. Hughson hid the linen in the garret. Then she took it out again after the first search to hide it under the stairs. She's real clever-like, so when the constables came back they missed it. Then later that night, I seen the mistress carrying it to her mother's house."

John Hughson leaped to his feet, interrupting. "She is a vile, good-for-nothing girl!" he shouted. "She had been got with child by her former master!"

Hughson hoped that his outburst might distract the court, but his bit of rumor was not the morsel in which this room was interested.

"Who else, young Burton?" the court demanded. "Who else took part in this nefarious plot? You are reminded, you are before a court of law, and your pardon depends on a complete testimony."

"Well, just yesterday morning I was sweeping the porch and I heard the Dutchman John Romme saying to my master, 'If you will be true to me, then I will be true to you.' To this my master replied, 'I will, and I will never betray you.' Which I found odd and suspicious, as such."

With this added revelation, examining the room and pondering his own situation, Hughson belatedly came to the realization that he was screwed, and it suddenly dawned on him how he had just managed to hurt his cause not only with the room but also with the one person who had the power to stop this madness. In a typical John Hughson style adjustment of strategy, before the entire audience to whom he had just defamed young Mary, Hughson instantly tried the opposite tactic of compliment and flattery.

"She was a very good girl," he cried, assuring those who were still bothering to listen. "Why, in hard weather last winter, she used to dress herself in me own clothes, put on boots, and go out with me in my sleigh in the deep snows into the commons to help me fetch firewood for my family. Love her like one of my own, really."

In response, the crowd stared back at Hughson, largely quiet. The ones that were making a sound giggled at his ineptitude.

"Silence, man!" the deputy town clerk ordered him. "Continue. Speak the truth."

"I hardly dare speak," Mary cringed back dramatically. "I am so much afraid I will be murdered by them!"

Hughson and the other accused were doomed and they knew it. If there was any doubt, the testimony that came next from John Vaarck, the baker—Caesar's owner—took that away as well. After demonstratively apologizing for the fact that he was too busy with work to enslave his Negro properly, Vaarck told a story that would further cement the fate of the accused.

That very afternoon, he said, his younger slave, Bastian, had met his master's growing anxiety about this recent trouble with a look of guilt of his own. "What do you know, boy?" the baker insisted he pressed him. They stood in the kitchen, where the slave boy slept on a mat in the corner.

" 'Nothing, sir,' " the baker said Bastian had offered sheepishly. " 'I don't know nothing.' "

"This is no time for nonsense. Have it out now, boy, before that black bastard, Caesar, has us all marched to the gallows."

Bastian thought that an excellent point. After apparently allowing the thought to settle, the boy pointed down to the floor below them.

"What? Something wrong with your bloody foot? Stop the riddles!"

"Look underneath the floor, sir. There's something down there."

Vaarck did indeed look down there. As far as he could tell, there was no trapdoor, no loose floorboard. In order to look underneath his kitchen, Vaarck had to walk out his house, climb through his neighbor's yard, then come alongside to stare into the small dark crevice beneath his home. Huffing, on his knees, Vaarck looked up at where Bastian stood behind him.

"And you just happened to come across this little hiding space, did you?"

Bastian shrugged back at his pink owner.

Reaching into the darkness, hoping not to find a handful of skunk or porcupine for his efforts, Vaarck's hand came on the texture of rough fabric atop the dry soil. As he pulled out the heavy bag, the contents clinked as they rubbed together. Plates, stolen linen, filled it.

That bastard Caesar, Vaarck said he thought. He'd spent good money on that darky, gave him damn near free rein, and this was how Caesar had repaid him.

What interested the court as much as the booty, which was brought out now for the three judges to see, was the location itself.

When questioned Vaarck told them, "The only way you can get down there is through the yard of John Romme." That neighbor whose yard the house and its kitchen adjoined was the very John Romme whom Mary Burton had just described as being in cahoots with John Hughson. The area was only accessible through Romme's small yard, Vaarck insisted. The implication: that even if his own slave had strayed, there were whites guilty of more than just loose management, to be discovered in this affair. John Romme was married into the Dutch upper class of the colony, but this allegation and implication of guilt was too much to ignore. Despite his high-up connections, John Romme was sent for immediately.

Not even adding another white suspect, this one a member of the old Dutch gentry, would be able to move John Hughson from the focus of the judicial eye. Considering the social relations and possible ramifications of prosecuting one of their own class for such a petty crime, if anything, an arrest of John Romme would make it more likely the Hughsons would be made the scapegoats, that the burden of blame could be carried by them completely. Fate dictated this to be the case, as the constables sent to retrieve Romme returned with the news that the gentleman had already absconded. Still, too much of a political bother, really, when you had a perfectly good (and perfectly guilty) white man to take the burden right in front of you. So it turned out that John Hughson was good for something after all.

Seeing his predicament, Hughson thought confession his best alternative, and proved to have much to offer to the conversation. He confided that Peggy had given him goods, and told him that they had been left by Caesar, a stash, Hughson admitted, he later delivered to his mother-in-law. He added that he proceeded to hide the silver coins through repeated visits to confound the investigation. He further went on to say that it was Peggy that gave him the remainder of the bundle, which he delivered that morning to the authorities.

The court scribe struggled to keep up with Hughson's guilty revelation, making sure the language was correct to ensure its legal worth. Finishing up the last words, the document was turned back to Hughson for his approval.

"Sign your confession, John Hughson. Your testimony will be noted," the court clerk told him on completion. Hughson just stared at the lengthy page, its ink still wet.

But now he declined to put his signature to the document.

"What? What are you on about?" the court demanded. "It's your confession, man. You agreed to give your confession; you've already told the room of your part in this matter, what is the point of resistance now? Don't be daft, sign the paper."

Hughson continued to stare at the words on the page, considering the matter. Then, coming to a decision, he shook his head at the whole thing. "No, I don't think I shall. No, not at all. Thank you anyway, gentlemen."

"Are you quite mad? Sign the paper!"

"There is no occasion for me to sign it," Hughson insisted.

The court was aghast at the insolence of this rascal. They were so busy voicing the outrage over this affront to the court that they didn't bother to discern that the reason John Hughson wouldn't sign the confession was in fact fairly practical. The old fool couldn't read even the simplest words on the page, even if he could have managed more than an X to add to them. He was illiterate.

Regardless, both John and Sarah were remitted right then and there, with the understanding that they would be brought back in front of the Supreme Court on the very first day of the next term.

The last white on trial, Peggy Kerry, had more fight to offer.

MAT JOHNSON

Despite the wealth of witnesses against her and the detailed confessions, Peggy stood on the witness stand unmoved, and unmoving.

"Do you, Peggy Kerry, admit to having had possession of the stolen property from Hogg's store?"

"I do not," the redhead resisted, her back straight despite the societal shame engendered in that room and foisted down upon her.

"You do not even admit to the repeated attempts to conceal the evidence from the rightful authorities, as already laid out by the confession of your landlord, John Hughson?"

"I most certainly do not." Peggy stood strong, ignoring the rumbling of the onlooking crowd.

"Will you admit, then," the court continued, "as it has already been revealed here this day, that you willingly have shared your bed with a Negro property of Vaarck, the baker, this notorious black called Caesar, that now stands bound in this courtroom?"

"I deny that as well," Peggy said to them, ignoring the motion off to her right when Caesar's shocked gaze snapped in her direction.

Focused on Peggy's eyes, Caesar silently begged a response as his lover forcibly tried to ignore him.

"You what?" the court continued. "Oh, I see you are being quite the villainess this day, miss. Then, may I ask, what fact is it that you would be willing to testify to this day?"

"Only to the goodness of my landlords, John and Sarah

Hughson," Peggy told the room. "They are honorable, decent people and I am fortunate to board with them," she said, looking over to where the Hughsons sat, making sure they heard her every recommendation. The stolen property was not the only treasure that had been removed from John Hughson's tavern to his mother-in-law's. Unknown to the court that day, Peggy's young son was waiting for her with the old woman as well. Her only son, in the hands of the people she was being asked to incriminate. Some said the boy was as white as any colonist's child, others that he had the African blood in him as sure as any other mulatto. Either way, Peggy knew her only chance of protecting him would be to hold her tongue as concerned the family that now had him.

After listening to his alleged sins revealed, his guilt reasserted, when called to testify, Caesar, too, denied all that involved him in the crime of the stolen property of Mr. and Mrs. Hogg. Not that his denial would mean much; any hope either he or Peggy held for being released on bail was now far gone. But when it came time to address the issue of his relationship with Miss Kerry, Caesar, his pride evidently still intact, and despite the sure knowledge of persecution such revelation would beg, was more forthcoming.

"Mary Burton told the truth, in that regard," Caesar told the room as Peggy took her turn to stare downcast.

He looked directly at her as he spoke, nonetheless. "I have been sleeping in the room of Peggy Kerry and I will not deny that," he said.

It was an admission that could surely cause his destruction, but Caesar stood proudly behind the pronouncement. Displaying the very defiance, stubbornness, and nihilism that soon would be revealed as archetypal of his brown brethren in response to their enslavement in New York City.

FIRE, FIRE, SCORCH, SCORCH,
A LITTLE, DAMN IT, BY AND BY

EXACTLY TWO WEEKS LATER, at one in the afternoon, things started getting hot. At Fort George, on the southern tip of Manhattan isle, the glow of fire danced on the roof of His Honor, Lieutenant Governor Clarke's house. The light show came to fruition before notice was even called to it. It started on the roof of the east side of the house, about twenty feet from the closest building, the chapel. By the time the alarm was sounded, the blaze had ignited the entire woodshingled rooftop, raging into a beacon that could be seen well beyond the city limits.

The fires had started.

The chapel's bell alerted the population at large to the conflagration. Soon the city's citizenry, never known for their general sense of community, interrupted their lives to come to the rescue. Fire was a communal event. The town's newly acquired state-of-the-art, side-stroking, manual-pump fire engine could divert some river water out its gooseneck onto a burning structure to slow some furies, but nobody thought that was enough, given the magnitude of the blaze. Once these wood-beamed structures really struck afire, the community's primary duty was reduced to removing all they could of the internal contents of the building, its destruction being a foregone conclusion. From practice, the approaching crowds knew how to set up a proper bucket brigade, to form lines to the doors, with at least one line carrying the building's prized possessions out into the safety of the street while another brought buckets of water in to slow the blaze. It was a group performance that was as practical as it was collective. Fire knows no satiation, and in a city with over eleven thousand people, where buildings had been erected so close together, if not handled immediately a fire such as this could easily grow beyond its initial source. Its hunger devouring an entire neighborhood without pause.

Much commended in the aftermath, the gathered crowd got most of the furniture out of the lieutenant governor's home before the blaze completely engulfed it. Fine couches brought from Europe met sooty hands in the chill late afternoon air. Oil portraits risked becoming little more than flammables. But what did it matter? Despite their efforts, despite the eventual arrival of the fire engines, it was soon determined that not the home, nor the chapel next door, could be saved. A violent southeast gale had goaded the flames faster than could be discouraged.

It was decided that efforts should be diverted instead to the secretary's office, situated right outside the English fort's gate, where the priceless records of the colony were kept, as well as the soldiers' barracks that stood across the quad from the governor's house. With speed and diligence born of desperation, the citizens stormed the buildings, throwing records and books out the windows on the town side to save them from destruction as the heaving winter wind blew documents chaotically down the city's streets. Most were later recovered, and it was a good thing, too, as soon after the office building was vacated, the roof became engulfed as well.

Chaos took hold as the contents of these rich structures were vomited, neighbors trying desperately in the confusion to save their city from destruction. As if nature wanted an inferno, the wind continued its mischief, draped with smoke and decorated with the floating red embers of civilization. Soon, too, the nature of man seemed to conspire for the blaze as well. When fire ignited the roof of the nearby military barracks, not long after it took the office building, the rumor spread through the crowd that there was now a greater danger that must be avoided: there was gunpowder in that building. The humble barracks was now on the verge of becoming the largest bomb any had had the misfortune of standing next to. As the new alarm spread, so did the crowd flee. Magically, the majority remembered previous engagements for which they were due, and silently slipped away into the shadows.

"People! Everyone! There is no greater danger! The barracks are empty! Come back!" pleaded the lieutenant governor, but his desperation only sent those he futilely addressed further. He was not exactly an objective source, was he? And so, without human impediment, the buildings were free to burn to the ground, and did so. After the military barracks and surrounding structures had collapsed to piles of char and ember, as feared, a collection of hand grenades suddenly exploded within the devastation.

When night fell and Mr. Cornelius Van Horne, captain of the local civilian militias, organized seventy armed men to go marching around the town, many just called him a madman. A paranoid fool, they said. Yes, the fire had taken down much of the military fort, but that was no cause for storming the streets, leading an armed band in circles till daybreak. Surely there was a less sensational reason behind the incident. The lieutenant governor had only just had his gutters cleaned by the plumber that morning. Was it not possible that an errant coal from his soldering iron's pot had started the inferno? Sure, the fire seemed to have started at several places along the roof at once, but no one could account for such things. Nothing to get hysterical about, nothing to see here. Everyone just go home.

Then, exactly a week later, a fire broke out midday near the bridge at the southwest end of town at the house of Captain Warren, brother-in-law to Chief Justice DeLancey. The fire engines came soon enough, and despite the fact that much of the roof had already been consumed, they were successful in dousing the blaze before more damage could be done. Again, it was a roof that ignited. Another fire so soon was not uncommon—so many wooden-roofed structures constructed with other flammable materials, combined with use of flame lighting, made fires a fairly common (if terrifying) event. Early inspection declared it to be the accidental firing of the chimney.

Then, exactly a week after that, for a third Wednesday in a row, fire struck the city once more, this time at the storehouse of Mr. Winant Van Zant. The site was on the east of town, an old wooden building filled with hay, the kind of building of which a fire would make an excellent meal. Van Zant's storehouse was closely connected to many other wooden buildings along the street and it seemed assured that all would be lost, that soon at least an entire block would become engulfed in the inferno. If it wasn't for the fact that the property sat on the slip by the East River, giving both the engines and bucket carriers a close and convenient source of water, it might have been a disaster, but in the end only one house was devoured. In the early moments, before the whispers and rumors slipped in with the accompanying fear, it was thought that a pipe smoker who'd been sitting by the hay was responsible. But then questions arose. Where had the fire started? How had it spread? If it started on the one side of the building, how was it the hay on the other side began to smolder almost simultaneously?

Then, three days after that, the now familiar fire alarm rang out once more, this time drawing people to the house of Mr. Quick and Mr. Vergeau in the downtown Fly Market. Upon running to the call, the fire was discovered to be in the middle of the cow stable behind the house, centered in a pile of hay. The fire was quickly extinguished, but as the tired, increasingly anxious colonists were returning to their lives, giving thanks that greater trouble had been averted, they were greeted by chilling alarm. Yet another blaze raged on this Saturday's dusk.

This time the flames arose from the westside house of Ben Thomas, next-door neighbor to Captain Sarly. So another military man's property was being threatened by the recent rash. The fire had apparently begun in the kitchen, and was only discovered because of its heavy smoke. Again it was successfully put out before greater damage could be done. The source was searched for and found to be in some straw near the bed of one of Ben Thomas's slaves. The whispers continued after the embers cooled. Who could be behind this? Spanish spies, perhaps? Surely it couldn't be one of our own. What if it was even worse than imagined? What if the slaves were involved?

And then, only a few hours later, early Sunday morning, pedestrians passing by the stables of Joseph Murray, Esq., on Broadway smelled a wooded smoke and, considering circumstances, decided to look further. Their inspection revealed a collection of dead coals left in the stable's piled feed. The dried hay around the coals had been singed, showing proof that the coals had been lit when laid there. It was the great fortune of Mr. Joseph Murray, Esq., and his many neighbors that the embers died before a true fire could be blown into existence. Here, again, great danger to the upper class of Manhattan was once more averted, as Murray's property was nestled in the bosom of an array of wealthy homes. The fire would have been provided an expensive sabbath breakfast at the expense of some of the most prominent colonists. Again, searching for clues, for some kind of understanding to belay or rationalize their growing trepidation, it was discovered that there was a trail of coal and ashes that led away from the nearby ignition site. Following the dark line back away from Murray's singed hay, an inspector arrived at the fence that led to the neighboring house that adjoined the stable. A stable inhabited by none other than this neighbor's slave. And wasn't he always a suspicious bastard?

A few hours later into the Sunday's midday, a lady, Mrs. Abigail Earle, was enjoying a cup of tea, taking the afternoon off from church services to relish the quiet day. After such a long winter, it was a luxury to simply relax by her open window and take in the spring breeze. And there were sights to see. With so many of the respectable colonists off at church, it was common to see their unruly slaves walking the streets with the boldness of the free, and one couldn't be too careful of these unsupervised Negroes these days. So it was with particular interest that she noted three bucks strolling casually down her street as if they owned the place (which they most certainly did not). One in particular had the devil in him. As she watched with growing disgust, she heard him speak with "a vaporing air" to the other two:

"*Fire, fire, scorch, scorch*, A LITTLE, *damn it*, BY AND BY," he said.

Then the darky threw up his calloused brown hands at his blithe statement, laughing bitterly. *Ha-Ha-Ha*, his joy as great as her horror.

And so it became official. For the good white citizens of the municipality of New York, it was now time to let the panic begin.

"LIBERTY!"

T HE EUROPEAN IMMIGRANTS of this little trading town at the base of the Hudson had good reason to fear that their African captives might be conspiring to burn down its buildings, terrorize its inhabitants, or worse. For one, the Africans had every right to. They were treated like animals, but they were humans: a slight contradiction. Slave revolts were a constant threat in the New York territory since its founding as a European outpost, from the first uprising in 1663 when Angolan slaves and poor whites banded together to fight in Gloucester County. Between the years 1687 and 1741, a slave plot erupted on average every two and a half years. In regard to these victims of an international atrocity, daily suffering the dehumanization and physical tortures of chattel slavery, the surprise was not that the Africans might be up to something, but that it didn't happen even more often. The uprising of 1712 had not faded from contemporary memory, and despite the steady enactment of stricter and stricter slave laws since the British seized the colony from the

Dutch decades before, there was also the common knowledge that the more strict the laws enacted, the more unrealistic their enforcement became. See here: the beginnings of white American fear. See here: the birth of the black boogeyman.

It should be noted as well that the colony on a whole was one that had seen its identity and nationality change dramatically in the last century, and certainly the battle for complete dominance of the New World was far from won by the English. In the immediate era, the constant and bloody struggle for dominance of the eastern Atlantic sea between the Spanish and the English had come to a head once again. In response to England's disregard for the Assiento—the Spanish international pact on slave importation—as well as tensions over the British logwooding off the Spanish-controlled Honduran coast, Spain was reacting with some lawlessness of her own. When Robert Jenkins, captain of the English ship *Rebecca*, held up his dried, pickled ear he'd had severed from his head by the Spanish at Parliament, he became a symbol for the reason's behind Britain's declaration of war in 1739, a conflict that became known as the "War of Jenkins' Ear." The two nations were, at the time of New York's provincial crisis, involved in a battle for the dominance of the Americas, a battle at that time raging in Florida over control of that Spanish-held territory, with the southern English colonies, like Georgia, embroiled in the fighting as well.

It was as a result of this war that six hundred of New York's troops were not stationed in the city at the time that these fires broke out. Instead, they had been sent south six months before for an attack on Cuba, leaving the city of New York with only a paltry military presence. When these fires erupted, New York was at its most vulnerable moment for armed takeover, whether from external forces or internal. It was also a well-known fact (or well-worn rumor) that the Spanish (as the French and English would do in later conflicts) was offering freedom to any African who would join their call to arms. Freedom + Negroes = trouble for white people.

Not far from the minds of virtually every white citizen of the day, before, and most certainly after the first occurrences of the New York fires, was the fear that this call to arms had evidently been answered by uprising Africans, with devastating results for the Europeans they happened to come upon.

On September 9, 1739, in South Carolina's Stono colony, an Angolan named Jemmy took to the streets with a crowd of other enslaved Africans, and together they started marching south, gathering more slaves, male and female, as they passed each household. Their ranks swelled to more than one hundred by nightfall. Small bands of Africans were known to have been escaping to Florida at the time, where they were promised to be rewarded not only with their freedom but also with parcels of land for their alliance. The Spanish had even released a proclamation to assure them that any slaves who deserted the English colonies to come to Saint Augustine would be likewise rewarded.

Similar to the situation arising in New York, it was also

thought that the enactment of tighter laws meant to further control the Africans might be a factor in the Negroes' increased resistance. The more suffocated the slaves were, the more desperate they seemed to breathe freedom. The passing of local security acts meant that soon all white males would be required to carry arms to church on Sunday, in response to the growing Negro threat.

Jemmy and his followers' march, later called the Stono Rebellion, took place on the Christian sabbath, Sunday being the traditional day of rest for European immigrants, regardless of religious temperament. This is why the band of Africans were able to get so far along their trail in the first place without encountering greater white resistance. As the Europeans prayed for their souls in the houses of their Lord, the freedom-seekers walked to reclaim their bodies, each step moving them further beyond bondage.

The march started started when, around two in the afternoon, a dozen slaves gathered in St. Paul's Parish by the Stono River, twenty miles outside Charlestown. Slipping into a gun shop, the slaves seized all merchandise, and immediately tested the firearms, shooting the two clerks working in the place.

Statement made and retreat no longer an option, the band then marched straight over to the house of Mr. and Mrs. Godfrey, killing both, and murdering their son and daughter as well. From there they kept moving, carrying banners that declared LIBERTY! Shouting the word over and over again, and drumming it as well. Pushing forward toward the promise of it.

It was nearly daybreak when they reached Wallace's tavern, sparing the proprietor's life solely because he was known to have been humane to his slaves. After that though, it got bloody, as the rebelling Africans took all lives in the next half-dozen houses they came upon.

Not all the slaves were willing participants: the ones belonging to Thomas Rose, for example, hid their master; they themselves were forced to join the growing mob or face similar fate to the whites.

Others, however, joined in eagerly. It was a dream incarnate. All those days staring beyond the master's fences, and wondering what was on the other side. The few whites the rebellion did encounter as it moved on were quickly released from the mortal coil. It was the one white they accidentally let get away, Lieutenant Governor Bull, who ran to spread the word of what was happening, and led a posse of British colonists back to squash the rebellion.

The whites, gathered and armed, found their former human property resting in a field not far from the Edisto River. The Africans had managed to get ten miles, killing about two dozen Europeans along the way. Near four that afternoon, the rebels got off two shots before the whites mowed them down in a hail of musket fire, quickly striking fourteen of the Africans dead. By nightfall, sixteen more would die, although at least thirty others had managed to run away, at least, for the moment. All would eventually be caught. And dealt with.

Could they have been that surprised at the outcome? They

were trying to walk, with just a few guns, all the way to Florida. In a rather productive day, they'd managed ten miles. There were two hundred and seventy miles more, through Savannah, and countless other white enclaves, all the way down the Atlantic coast, between them and freedom.

Insanity.

Or maybe the Stono Rebellion, and really all of the African rebellions that took place in America over the three centuries that saw slavery, were less about the literal attainment of freedom than the ephemeral symbol of it. That it was worth the price of one's very existence to shake off a lifetime of brutalization, and walk upright and uncompromising as a full human being, if only for a fleeting moment.

Eventually there was a growing silence among the Africans as they walked south, after questions and small talk had been eliminated, as the growing reality that they were marching to their death came to realization. Repeated were the indignations rained upon them, relieved to speak outside, and in full voice of their mistreatment. Reflections on moments of joy and pleasure, summarizing lives soon to be drawn to conclusion. At the end of their march, when they'd arrived at that large open field that late afternoon, it seemed a good place to meet one's maker. In the early fall warmth it was a pleasure to sit in the tall grass after the long march, to take off the shoes that now constricted. To wiggle brown toes and stare up to see a sky above them at its last appearance in their life. Taking a moment to rest before their fate caught up to them, listening to the wrens as its harbinger. Putting their spiritual houses in order so that when their certain death came, they were prepared to welcome it.

Though written off as mere shortsighted stupidity by some whites, the uprising was something much more complicated: desperation to its suicidal, murderous extreme. It was this nihilism, this complete absence of restraint, regardless of self-preservation, that made the possibility of slave rebellion so terrifying to the white colonists. Uprisings had a myriad of practical repercussions that made them so dreaded, but it was also, in part, this very attitude that made these incidents so terrifying. That the Africans knew they were going to die from the moment they chose to be defiant. That they didn't care. As long as they dragged down enough whites with them.

THE SPANISH NEGROES

A T TEN A.M. on the morning of Monday, April 6, 1741, yet another fire broke out, this time at the home of Sergeant Burns, starting supposedly in his chimney though he insisted the flue had been swept just days before. Then a fire broke out on the roof of Mrs. Hilton's home on the corner of the Fly Market, another house that adjoined the residence of Captain Sarly, evidence left behind that it, too, had been intentionally set.

Could anyone be surprised? Captain Sarly's neighbors seemed to be particularly unfortunate. Surely this could not be coincidence; there are no coincidences in a world of fear.

"It's his slave, it must be. The black beast is always saying he should be a free man, isn't he?"

"The impertinence!"

"Saying he was kidnapped off his Spanish ship and enslaved. I heard Captain Sarly paid good money for him and the other Spanish Negroes, from a reputable trader. Got a bill of sale and everything."

The enslaved, Juan, was soon caught on the street, and quickly surrounded. The crowd demanded an answer of him. "Talk, villain! Do you or do you not know the source of these fires?"

"So now you care to know what I know," Juan responded. "I know you best look elsewhere." His tone read by the assembled mob as pure insolence. Juan was less talkative after he'd been summarily beaten and dragged to jail.

It was a dirty, open secret that since the 1680s, when British privateers captured Spanish ships, a profitable habit was made of selling darker-skinned sailors into slavery in New York. Juan was part of a group of Africans kidnapped, just a few years before, by Captain Lush. Despite insistence of their free status, for lack of legal documentation, the group was declared human property by the admiralty and sold into slavery in homes across Manhattan. Not surprisingly, these Spanish-speaking Africans were notoriously bitter. When you included that the dark group spoke among themselves in a foreign tongue, that slave or not, they were chosen citizens of a dominion of the Vatican and its papal plans, in the eyes of the white colonists of New York City the Spanish Negroes were even less deserving of trust than the rest of the feared African hoard. If one of this suspicious band was involved in the suspicious fire, surely the others were in cahoots as well.

"The Spanish Negroes! The Spanish Negroes!" was the

call cried out by the frightened whites. "Take up the Spanish Negroes!"

And taken up they were.

To label a person (or group) a scapegoat implies a judgment of guilt or innocence. It implies a tacit accusation against the accuser. It says what you are doing is blaming an innocent person, based solely on prejudice or convenience. But scapegoating offers more subtle pleasures as well. Don't forget the release of fear provided, freedom from anxiety through the abandonment of reason. The great thing about scapegoating is that you don't even have to believe its victim is responsible for the action in question. You just have to pretend you do, and it still makes you feel better. No more fires to worry about here, we've captured the Spanish Negroes now. The Spanish Negroes did it. The Spanish Negroes will pay for their crime. When you get hit, you hit back—the question of whether you hit the right person, or for the right reasons, or whether the entire action will have any effect on the situation is irrelevant. What's important is that the issue has been addressed. What's important is that when there's a crime, someone pays for it—who pays matters less than the debt to society. As long as that debt is paid, you can all rest, pacified. Because, let us acknowledge, it was never about the crime as much as your fear of it.

★   ★   ★

The Spanish Negroes were herded from across the colony, caught up and brought to City Hall for questioning by the magistrates. It was a little after four in the afternoon, and the justices gathered from their workaday lives, for once not bothered to be pulled from their commerce. The esteemed men were proceeding to the judicial building relieved, at last, to have someone from whom they could demand an explanation— DING DING DING DING DING—yet another fire alarm bell frantically rang out.

Dear God, when would the horror cease?

Searching out the cause for alarm, scouring rooflines for the source of the smoke above, a small streak of flame was seen running up the shingles of Colonel Philipse's roof.

"Blimey, from the look of it, this fire must have started on the side of the roof that faced *against* the wind," noted one white onlooker with dread.

The ignition point meant it was highly implausible, if not impossible, that this fire was a mere accident. Even more suspicious, the fire seemed to have started strategically in the middle of three large wooden storehouses. These buildings had no chimneys and were too far removed from any other structure to have been caused by a random spark. No, again, this must be arson. There was no other explanation.

The colonists were still busy extinguishing this conflagration, which they had now concluded could only have been started in the building's interior, when the cry of "FIRE!!!" was heard yet again. With the storehouse blaze virtually subdued, the majority of the crowd ran off immediately in this new direction to tackle the next crisis. With the bulk of the crowd gone, and the fire, for all intents and purposes, well contained, there were only a few colonists left at the storehouse to comb over the dying embers. One of the men climbed on top of the building to extinguish anything left still burning directly from that precarious vantage point. It was risky business, but expedient, dumping his bucket down on the last of the smoldering embers. *Don't bloody fall*, was primarily what he was reminding himself, when through the smoke this brave soul noticed movement below. Behind the house, shielded from the view of those still on the ground, he espied the dark visage of a man. And the ebony phantom was scurrying *away* from the fire. From his rooftop vantage, the colonist saw this dark apparition jump out of a storehouse window onto the ground far below. Not just any man, the running man could now be seen clearly, and he was: a Negro! The African was hopping away with desperate speed, hastily jumping over the fences of the small colonial yards as he fled.

"A Negro!" the white man on the roof called to the whites below.

Those on the ground looked up at him in confusion.

What are you going to do with a Negro? they seemed to be asking. Don't you mean, "A bucket of water, please"?

"A Negro! A Negro!" the man on the roof persisted in yelling down at them until the others finally seemed to get it.

"The Negroes are rising! The Negroes are rising!"

The chant now rose quickly through the crowd. Finally finding ready voices among them, ready believers. Word spreading almost as rapidly as the fires had. Fear becoming fact even before the facts actually emerged. The cry of the *"Negro"* becoming more specific as whites who had just seen this suspect tearing through their yards joined the chorus with sure identification of the culprit.

"Cuff Philipse, Cuff Philipse!" the mob chanted the fleeing black man's slave name.

He had been identified as none other than Cuffee, the enslaved of the prominent owner of the burned storehouse in question.

Soon the gathering mob stormed the house of Adolph Philipse in search of his human property. Cuffee was found at his master's door, wide-eyed, a-gawk at the white crowd, in possible confusion and definite fear.

"What were you doing by the fire?" they clamored.

"Why were you running? What were you running from?"

"Who else is involved?"

"Who is responsible?"

A barrage of questions were yelled, but opportunity afforded not one answer. Instead, the terrified Cuffee was dragged from his enslaver's home as his muscles struggled for release. The mob grabbed frantically at pieces of him, hit whatever resisted. It was thus that the battered Cuffee would arrive at the magistrates, borne on the shoulders of those who kept him alive only for answers.

The Negroes are rising! What had been the frantic ranting of an excited, frightened man on a smoke-enveloped roof, haunted the minds of the individuals who now comprised this new force of emotion that was the mob. The Negroes are rising!

Rising: being down, and trying to get up.

What a frightening prospect for those on top, indeed.

Isn't "the other" always a scary thing? That person you don't know, nor can decipher. The further their difference from your own, the more alien their food, the smell of their breath, their perspiration, the odd way their mouth forms the most common of words . . . the more they are something to fear, something to counter. The other is different, and that crime is obvious. What other parts of its nature are hidden? Wouldn't the unknown be capable of the unimaginable?

It wasn't long before the mob had changed their focus to a new target. Who were the seditionists? they were forced to ask themselves. The insurrection, such as it was, could not simply be emanating from the Spanish Negroes, that foreign, hostile threat. Nor could such rebellion, under any stretch of the imagination, be limited to one slave. Not even a loathsome Negro, such as Cuffee, no matter how ornery and foul his nature.

No! It was all of the black bastards, the enemy that lived in their very homes.

Blacks were an easy target to hit, particularly for an entity so indiscriminate. No need to wait for those already in captivity to confess to their sins when there was an abundance of Africans walking the streets that could be yanked by their necks by New York's concerned white citizens, molested into passivity, and booted through the doors of the local jail with the rest of them.

Let chaos ensue. Let no black be spared, even those who had just minutes before been helping the colony by passing water buckets and rescuing personal wealth they could never own. Being black on the streets of New York was enough to qualify for suspicion. The disregarding of what little rights the slaves had was no great cost for the cessation of white fear. The Africans were in this country solely to serve the Europeans anyway.

Cuffee was left to stew in his jail cell overnight before the official interrogation was to begin. It would have been a long night, too, high on anxiety and extremely low on comfort. As one colonist described his own stay in these accommodations some years later, "[N]othing but a bare floor to lay on— no covering—almost devour'd with all kinds of vermin." It could not even be called a fleabag cell because that would imply there was an actual bag to sleep on. Not that Cuffee could really sleep anyway, given the circumstance. Given what he knew must surely lay in front of him.

A prison in the colonial world is an expensive indulgence to spend on those in society least deserving of its funds. The cost of the building alone was prohibitive, but when you added the cost of maintenance it became a complete extravagance. Food had to be bought, prepared, and delivered. Fresh water had to be pumped and made available. Wood had to be chopped and stoked on the coldest of winter nights. And of course, someone had to be paid to make sure those inside never got out. In a colony based around commercial interests, where ambitious members of the British working class could scarcely be attracted to come in the first place, finding a white man content to spend his life babysitting the low life was impractical. The modern prison system that would be born decades later in that Quaker city to the south simply didn't exist yet. And even then, incarceration was too damn expensive. As said, New York has always been a city based around making money. So New York had no real prison in 1741, just the jail. Nobody had the time, or desire, to waste time policing, not if there was money to be made.

The criminal punishments of the era reflect that this was a colony that was economically focused, as opposed to morally driven. Whites who committed societal misdemeanors were punished in their purses. If convicted, whites could post a bond of good behavior, their fortunes being held ransom to ensure their future actions. Some were simply fined outright, occasionally losing their entire estate for severe crimes. Those without means could find themselves sold into indentured servitude, literally working off their debt to society. It always came down to money in New York, and what was most cost effective, boiling down to what the majority of Europeans in this society cared about most. Money was the reason they had left their old lives a continent away in the first place. But when it came to discipline for severe crimes, or discipline of enslaved Africans who were both penniless and whose humanity was seen to be of the lowest sort along the Great Chain of Being, the realities of colonial punishment were much more harsh.

The punishments meted were physical, fast, and dramatic. That was the attraction of public torture and execution. Instead of taking decades to punish a convicted criminal for his crime, the matter could be over in hours. Even minutes.

For non-capital offenses, the common punishment was flogging with a rod, or whipping. That would do you. This would take place in a public place, usually on a market day so you could get a good crowd for both the prisoner's humiliation and to serve as a warning to others. In one instance of the period, constables marched an insolent slave through the entire metropolis, giving him a lash at each intersection. Quite the tour of the city, it was. A far cry from a mere spanking, it was standard for a flogging to last for at least thirty-nine lashes. Death from shock or infection happened all the time. The humiliation alone was more than some could bear. In 1743, one sensitive would-be whipping post victim cut his own throat to avoid the horror of the lash.

For many others, a pillorying was their equally morbid fate. Marched into stocks, the convicted was required to stick his head, hands, and sometimes feet into the wooden pillory, which was then locked down in place. This made the pilloried fairly accessible, not to mention vulnerable when the crowd started throwing rocks and animal shit at their head, which of course the onlookers did. Once the crowd had exhausted its arsenal, then came the bad part. For the finale, they cut off the convict's ear. This last bit was a true crowd-pleaser, provoking victorious cheers from the thrilled spectators. After that, they let them go. It was possible afterward to still hear in that ear-hole okay (if it didn't get infected), but still. Nobody wants to be known as the crooked arse with the hole in their head for the rest of their lives, do they?

The destruction of public property was never a casual event in New York, regardless of the 1741 affair. Prior to 1750, 71 percent of those convicted of stealing got a good flogging for their efforts. Ten percent of these thieves were killed for their crime. This would only get more severe as the century progressed, with 22 percent executed, 26 percent whipped, and 28 percent branded for their crime. Even if you made it out with both ears after being caught and punished, there were often additional prices to pay. For example, not rarely, the letter *T* was burned into the thieves' forehead so that the world could see their guilt from then on.

So Cuffee had a fairly accurate idea what awaited him if they found him guilty, and that the word *if* was probably an overly optimistic one. There would be little weight given to his word, and even less to his human rights. In fact, Cuffee would be held for eleven days before his interrogation would even begin. By then it was known that, in addition to his initial identification and his presumed guilt, some whites had actually stepped forward and provided favorable depositions as well.

"I was working with him, all day," a young man offered. "He only left me a moment before the second fire bell, so he couldn't have lit the first fire."

"How was he acting?" the investigators asked incredulously. "Was there any suspicious behavior?"

"No, as I say, he was right here, working as always. Of course, when the first fire went up I asked him if he was going to help with buckets at his master's storehouse, and the Negro declined, if you can believe it."

"He what?"

"He said, 'I've had enough of being out in the morning.' Just like that, and walked off for a rest. But then, the Negroes are a lazy breed, you know."

Still other witnesses had Cuffee right at his master's door before the fire bell rang. One man who'd known Cuffee for years said that the slave was right next to him, watching the fire, but this fellow was old and his eyesight was piss poor on a clear day. The Negroes all looked so much alike anyway, how could the ancient white man really tell the difference? And even if all of the witnesses were correct and reliable, with slow burning, strategically placed embers, it was impossible for a timeline to be drawn that could prove absolute innocence. Cuffee could have placed the coals there early in the morning, or even the night before.

The difficulty of uncovering any good conspiracy is that, for all the suspicion one can have, its discovery still depends largely on getting those involved in the actual events to talk. Of course, these are usually the individuals least likely to blabber; even if they are not connected directly. Who would want to link themselves to a scheme so horrifying that any whose name is mentioned might lose their life? So for investigators, ways must be found, methods and strategies discovered, to get those involved to talk. There are those out there who might not even realize that they have a piece of information that could connect into the puzzle. So a bounty was set, one that said much about the society of the period. For whites with information, a reward of one hundred pounds was offered. For free Africans, mulattos, and Indians with information, it would be forty-five pounds. For slaves, divulging information would mean freedom plus twenty pounds, with an additional twenty-five pounds allocated for their masters. This, too, might serve as a seductive source of income among the lowest to better themselves, as opposed to the opportunities for theft, advantaged by some during the latest pandemonium of the fires.

And there *had* been a lot of stealing of late. When better to make an illicit acquisition than during the chaos of smoke and fear, when prized possessions were strewn by strangers' hands into the street? The theft of evacuated property was such a significant issue, the need to enforce order among the colonists so strong, that the magistrates and militia were sent to search out every home for stolen goods. While invading the space of people's houses, investigators were also encouraged to look for strangers to the colony who might be secretly responsible for the madness—surely so much destruction could not be instigated solely by one of New York's own. Yet in spite of the full onslaught of force, aside from one old slave, Cuba, and his equally elderly wife, who were arrested for owning more than they could afford, nothing nefarious was discovered.

★ ★ ★

It is unknown whether Mrs. Abigail Earle collected her hundred pounds for the information, but the impudent Negro she heard declaring, "*Fire, fire, scorch, scorch,* A LITTLE, *damn it,* BY AND BY," as his hands circled his head was identified as Quack (enslaved by Mr. Walter), and taken into custody.

After being summarily left to stew in his fear for a few days, Quack was brought to the magistrates for questioning.

"Slave Quack," began the interrogation, "you have been quoted as saying, 'Fire, Fire, Scorch, Scorch, a little, damn it, by and by' by a respected member of this community. There is no use denying it. So what say you to this line?"

"Oh, your honor. You know Quack didn't mean nothing by that; I love the Englishman. Matter of fact, I was remarking to my mates about the taking of Porto Bello by that Admiral Vernon, what had just happened before. Fine seaman, he is, why he taught them Spaniards something. Them Spaniards, they can't stand to a good Englishman, no sir. Like I was telling my associates, Admiral Vernon just burned them off slow, one by one. That's how him and them admirals did it."

The court paused to look at itself, confused. This was not the answer they were expecting. Surely the recent adventures of Admiral Vernon were something to marvel at, but still . . . the Negro had thrown them.

"A cunning excuse, slave Quack, this we will admit, but that is all the benefit we will give you. Perhaps some abler heads have planted this story in yours?"

Quack shrugged, offering what he could only hope was a portrait of innocent confusion to the room.

"Fine. Fortunately, we have benefit of the presence of your slave companions on that day in our custody as well. So let's see what these men of your own complexion have to say on the matter."

The other slaves were called for, and sheepishly they arrived, hands bound, petrified, shuffling forward as if blows were imminent.

"You, the accused, what do you say in regard to the conversation you were so suspiciously engaged in?" the judge demanded of them.

The oldest of the bunch, and the least frozen of the men, looked to his fellow prisoners before offering explanation.

"Well, sir, we was just walking about, marveling at how that Admiral Vernon was showing the Papists what's what. That this was but a small feat to what this brave officer would do by and by and . . ."

The court looked on, impressed with the testimony. It could mean only this one thing, and they all knew it.

"Enough," the judge silenced him. Turning to Quack, who for the moment was daring to believe himself cleared of the evidence, the judge continued. "Do you really expect this court to believe that your overheard comments are mere coincidence? Coming as they do, *a mere eighteen days* after the fort was burned to the ground? This alone is enough to damn you, but your hands give more. As Mrs. Earle has described, you lifted them up in the air and swept them in a circle around your head as you made this pronouncement. It is obvious that you were talking about our fair colony, and the fires that would engulf us.

The fact that you said 'by and by' gives testament that there would be more to follow. Your laughter then comes back to haunt you now, does it not? You have shown the blackness of your heart for all to witness. The gall, that you would not just talk of the white destruction, but rejoice in it! That your stories match proves that this is an organized plot indeed. And a higher intelligence must be behind your actions."

The lieutenant governor ordered a watch kept that evening, and that watch would stay on guard through the spring and into the summer. No precaution could be spared with the threat of revolt and rebellion so near.

ENEMIES OF THEIR
OWN HOUSEHOLD

A SLAVE IN ITSELF is not a person, not a human being. Slaves are simply beasts, commodities. Even the way we brand them with the stigmatizing noun *slave* as opposed to the literal adjective *enslaved* removes room for context and humanity.

The enslaved Africans of eighteenth-century New York left behind few records of their history, because, of course, that's what their captors intended. To reach back to them, to identify their stories and herald their sorrow is an act of rebellion in itself. To understand the Great Negro Plot, to discover the truth behind the innuendo of the time, we must move past the European arrogance that defined the period, in order to view the Africans of New York themselves.

The single most important text in regard to the the Great Negro Plot is a book called *The New York Conspiracy*, written in 1744, only three years after the incident's conclusion. The book is an exhaustive, detailed account of the events, offered in chronological order, and using actual trial proceedings, complete with depositions, confessions, and the notes of the magistrates and lawyers. By itself, it is a fascinating and thorough look at a peculiar event in history. If *The New York Conspiracy* hadn't been compiled by colonist Daniel Horsmanden, the plot might have faded completely into historical footnote.

Horsmanden was the perfect person for the task. He was one of the main judges/prosecutors involved in the events, and the court recorder. It would be difficult to find a more biased filter for information on the event at hand, yet because Daniel Horsmanden was so confident that his full accounting of the facts would prove to the world the just nature of the court, he delivered the text without any self-editing. Read carefully, the self-righteous Horsmanden often unwittingly incriminates what he is trying to defend. His interpretation and choice of relayed events is shaped by his bias, and is usually self-serving and transparent. That said, Horsmanden is generally honest, and the man does not shrink away from giving information that exposes his position. Still, while central to understanding the events of the Great Negro Plot, Horsmanden's narrative is heavily filtered through the white racial imagination of the period. It centers on dates and the orders of events, but doesn't offer us the opportunity to ask questions beyond the interest of the prosecution. Nor does it offer us the chance to hear the Africans' stories, only the ones they offered to a hostile court. To successfully skip beyond that court, to go directly to the source of the African community of the period, we must speak directly to the dead themselves.

In 1991, two hundred and fifty years after the Great Negro Plot took place, construction began on a new federal office building in lower Manhattan. Beneath the site of the proposed three-hundred-million-dollar project was discovered the three-hundred-year-old African Burial Ground, which once provided a resting place for New York's enslaved community. While the burial ground's existence was not a complete surprise—scholars of the city had never forgotten it was there—the exact location was enough of a mystery that the federal agency proved unprepared for the discovery. This place of rest, which sat on what was once the northernmost outskirts of the city, was in use from the late 1600s to 1796, although the African dead, much like the African living, were never given much of a "rest" by their European neighbors. In fact, in the middle of the eighteenth century while the cemetery was still in active use, whites built up pottery and tanning industries directly abutting it, using the site to dump their toxic refuse. Worse, medical students at New York Hospital were known to regularly steal black corpses for use as cadavers. After the cemetery was ordered closed, Dutch Americans built homes around the six-acre site and drilled outhouse ditches directly into the African Burial Ground so that for generations they were, literally, defecating on the dead.

But things had changed in Manhattan since those bad old days. While the white majority still could not be counted on to treat the African dead with reverence, the descendants of Africa were now strong enough to demand better. Initially, the federal government was hoping to quickly abide by the rules of the National Historic Preservation Act of 1966 and have their own archeologists swiftly excavate the site so that they could begin construction overtop the cemetery—thus completely destroying it. What they did not count on was a politically powerful, radicalized, astute black community that insisted, instead, that the government comply with another part of the 1966 law that required basic preservation of the historic site, along with public commentary and decision on how the landmark would be dealt. For once, the buried Africans had a stroke of good fortune, and it didn't hurt their cause that the city of New York at the time was under the administration of its first black mayor.

What the old African Burial Ground provided to contemporary black New York City was a lost connection to its history, a chance to grieve for the atrocities of the past and mourn for the nameless who came before them. With numerous blessing ceremonies, candlelight vigils, and readings, it was an opportunity to reaffirm the dignity of the disrespected. For a community whose culture and history were systematically stripped from them—particular their connection to Africa— it served as the missing link to a forgotten past.

For historians, once the site was treated with the complete respect it deserved, the burial ground offered an immense bounty: the chance to see firsthand the physical evidence of lives once denied their stories. The skeletal remains speak volumes. For enslaved blacks, an American childhood was extremely harsh, with mortality rates twice that of whites in the colony. Half of the skeletal children showed evidence of metabolic disease, indicating anemia, and growth retardation as well as defects in dental enamel because of starvation and disease. Based on the research done on other African burial grounds, including sites in Philadelphia, Maryland, Virginia, and South Carolina, historians have already concluded that African-American slaves during this period had the highest frequency of developmental defects of any observed human population, owing to malnutrition and disease. A comparison study of the teeth from the site conducted by the official research team at Howard University, however, found that the people at New York's African Burial Ground had less than half the adult instances of tooth defects as did the slaves of other colonies. What this discovery suggests is that a large portion of the Africans living in Manhattan were not native born, instead spending their childhood in Africa before being enslaved and shipped to the Americas. This is backed up by the shipping records of the period, which show many direct importations from West Africa to New York, particularly of those the Europeans called "Koromantines" or "Coromantees," slaves shipped from Fort Coromantee, off the coast of modern-day Ghana. The other group identified in the 1712 revolt, the Pawpaw, were, more than likely, Africans taken from another large slave port further east at Grand Popo, in modern-day Benin. Slave forts such as these served as way stations for people kidnapped from a variety of different regions and ethnicities further inland, marched for weeks to be brought to the coast for sale. While many enslaved shared larger ethnic affiliation (such as the widespread Akan people of the area), Coromantee and Pawpaw were not ethnic groups, but corporate designations, referencing the people they had been kidnapped by. They were brand names for the colonial buyers, like Sunkist or Chicken of the Sea.

The presence of Africa in colonial New York can also be seen in the names of its captives: Cuffee, Quash, Quack, and Quaco. The syllables were deformed by the contemporary European tongue, yet still they remain decipherable. Despite the habit among the Europeans of destroying the cultural vestiges of these African people, traditional names were often indulged and encouraged. This was largely practical: How embarrassing would it be to name your bestial slave "Phillip" only to receive a letter the next month that your brother had named his first son the same? Many of these slave names, like Quack, for instance, were actively encouraged because the Europeans found them utterly comic. (The duck says: Quack, quack, quack.) However, these names are actually the simply misunderstood derivations of Akan day names. In the Fanti dialect: Monday is Kwadjo; Tuesday, Kwabena; Wednesday, Kwaku; Thursday, Yao; Friday, Kofi; Saturday, Kwame; and Sunday, Kwasi. Or, in the even more familiar Ashanti dialect of Akan: Kojo, Kobina, Kwaku, Yao, Kofi, Kwame, and Kwesi. So, through the untrained ears of the Europeans, the names became distorted: Kofi became Cuffee; Kwadjo became Quash; Kojo became Cato, Cajoe, or Cudjo; Kwaku became Quaco and Quack.

Further physical evidence was found at the African Burial Ground. Etched into the coffin lid of a particular statuesque colonial African (who measured in at a whopping five foot nine) was the Sankofa, an Akan symbol literally meaning "Go and fetch," and figuratively, "You must look to the past to understand the future." Other bodies were found to have been buried with great care, along with quartz crystal beads and shells, that point to various African burial traditions.

Beyond the rotten, malformed teeth, the enslaved bodies unearthed at the African Burial Ground showed a multitude of signs of hard use. The majority of the skeletons unearthed revealed evidence of muscle enlargements around the legs, arms, and neck: a direct result of frequent strains due to heavy lifting, particularly the lifting of large weights balanced atop the skull in traditional African style. These slaves were not simply being forced into an active physical lifestyle by their captors, providing the foundation of domestic labor that built the colony, these Africans had been pushed to the limit of the human capacity. The deep bone lesions evident in most of the unearthed skeletons are typically caused by muscle tears from overstraining the human body. While the African technique of carrying objects on the head is an efficient, ancient practice, it seems that in the colony it was pushed beyond any reasonable limits, evidenced by the frequent examples of arthritis in the neck. Six of the remains uncovered at the African Burial

Ground showed ring-shaped fractures at the base of the skull, resulting from the spine shooting through and breaking a hole in the skull base, presumably from carrying staggering weights. This injury would have resulted in death, these slaves crushed under the burden of their bondage.

This harsh physical treatment was in no way limited to the adult men in bondage. Both men's and women's bones evidenced large muscle attachments as a result of harsh labor. While digging up the site, it was common for the Howard University technicians to uncover bones so thick that they would have been wrongly identified as male if other evidence of gender hadn't been present. Nor was the life of a slave any easier for young children. In fact, 50 percent of slave children died before the age of twelve, and 35 percent of that group didn't even make it out of infancy. Rickets and porotic-hyperostosis caused by vitamin D deficiency and anemia were common, as well as premature cranial closing. One child's body showed severe dental deformities probably caused by its mother's sick pregnancy, as well as anemia and lesions on the bones from infections. The top bones in the skeleton's neck were fused *solid* from carrying repeated heavy loads. Despite its harsh use in life, the corpse was interred gently in a pinned shroud by the people of his community.

But what of the flesh that once stuck to these bones? Or the clothes that kept that flesh warm? Bones are well and good for facts of life, but they don't offer a vision of the living people in question. For that, an excellent source of information is again, ironically, the group who most actively ignored and obscured the Africans' humanity during their lifetimes: the slave owners. Looking at the advertised notices for runaway slaves found in the newspapers of the day, we find detailed descriptions of the slaves, their physical appearances, and habits.

For example, from August 26, 1734, in the *New-York Weekly Journal*:

Run away from Johanna Kelsall of the City of New York, a Negroe Man known by the Name of Johnsey here in Town, but he writes his Name Jonathan Stow, about 25 Years of Age, of short Stature, bandy Legs, blubber Lips, yellow Complexion, his Hair is neither right Negro nor Indian, but between both, and pretty long, he had on when he went away a homespun jacket, a pair of Trowsers, and a speckled Shirt.

Whoever takes up the said Negro and secures him, or brings him to his Mistress, shall have 40 Shillings Reward and all Reasonable Charges paid by me.

So here we have a man who refuses to be named by those who enslave him, insisting instead on his own identity separate from the one imposed on him. This is a man who displays a mix of ethnic features, most notably African. If his hair was neither fully African nor Indian, did that mean he was a mix between the two? Considering his light skin color and New York's history, it was more likely that Jonathan Stow was ethnically mixed with European blood as well. So was such a common mixture too shameful to mention in the advert, or was this racial reality not even considered in lieu of the hypocrisy of the moment?

From December 19, 1737, the *New-York Gazette*:

Ran away from John Bell, of New York City, carpenter, one Negro woman Jenney, 14–15 years, born in *New York*, speaks English and some Dutch. She has a flat Nose, thick Lips, and full faced; had on when she went away, a Birds eyed Waistcoat and Pettycoat of a darkish colour, and a Callico Waistcoat with a large red flower, and a broad stripe, a Callico Pettycoat with small stripes and small red flowers. Whoever shall take up said Negro Wench and bring her to said John Bell, or secure her and give Notice, so that he can have her again, shall have *Three Pounds* as a Reward, and all reasonable charges.

At the beginning of womanhood, Jenney would be just old enough to make running away a practical idea. So then you must ask, had she planned to run away when she reached the first stage of adulthood, or had her entry into adulthood made running away a necessity? From the descriptions of her clothes, flowers and all, her lot was not as harsh as most of her caste, so she may have received some favor. It is possible, of course, that her enslaver John Bell might have been looking at Jenney with too favorable an eye as her body blossomed, a position many a young female slave found herself in.

This slave notice appeared on August 18, 1746, in the *New-York Weekly*:

Run away on Sunday the 10th instant from Captain George Hall, of this city, a tall likely young Negroe man named Quaw; he is a cunning artful fellow, Jamaica born, stutters very much and has one of his ears cropt; stole away £5, 12s, and £3 Johannes Pieces and was seen going towards Knightbridge. Whoever takes up said Negro and brings him to his master, shall have fifty shillings reward and all reasonable charges paid by George Hall.

At a time when European colonists assume the intellectual inferiority of the African, we get a description of Quaw as "cunning artful." The name "Quaw" implies an African origin, another derivative of "Kwaku" perhaps. Quaw's ear had been cropped. It is possible this was the result of an accident, or some slaver's plantation brand. Ear clipping was also the sort of punishment appropriate for a failed runaway attempt in the past. At least Quaw was smart enough to steal back some of his nonexistent wages before hitting the road this time.

Viewed individually, these markers of the past are fascinating glimpses into elusive stories. In a life of abuse, what was the incident that made each run? How far did they get, and how did they meet their conclusion? In a larger sense, looking over the multitude of notices posted in and about the New York and New Jersey settlements in the 1730s, '40s, and '50s, a larger picture reveals itself through the overlaying descriptions left behind. A smallpox epidemic during the lifetime of these slaves is evident in the numerous descriptions of the "pock-broken" skin on the runaways. Incidents of branding are evident, as two slaves in 1730 both had the letters *RN* burned into their shoulders. Scarring from the whip seems a common occurrence, as well as signs of the kind of excessive labor their bones would show centuries later, with descriptions of disjointed limbs occurring frequently. There are also similarities among the runaways that might be exemplary of the type who could indulge in that form of resistance: most runaways, not surprisingly, are young and male. Many are described as native born, which would give them an advantage in navigating the region. Along this line, several are described as mulatto, with repeated mentions of Indian hair or Indian mix, which might be the literal truth, but again, was probably a way of pointing at the mixed race of a slave without acknowledging the European blood that was part of the equation.

Their clothes—so important for identification considering that new garments were difficult to come by during the era—were mostly of coarse, cheap, homespun cloth, with variety being the exception. Brass buttons were a common part of the runaway slave ensemble. For men, felt hats are featured frequently in their descriptions, as well as breeches, stockings, and buckled shoes. For women, calico (then meaning white cotton) waists and petticoats appear as frequently. Another item that many slaves took along with them on their freedom runs were their violins—the boom boxes of the era. Testaments are often given of escaped Africans' musical abilities with these instruments. The violin was a beloved source of entertainment, but it could also serve as a possible source for income as well, particularly for people who might have to beg for survival. Well acclimated into New York life, several of the runaway slaves spoke Dutch in addition to English, reflecting the languages used in the fine households in which they were held in bondage.

In the urban setting of New York, slaves lived largely in the wealthier sections of the city, being themselves one of the primary symbols of their captors' fortune. Inside these great homes, however, their accommodations were the opposite of luxury; they were usually forced to sleep on the floor of the same kitchen in which they'd spent all day working, or were vulnerable to the elements in narrow, poorly insulated attic crawlspaces. At the beginning of the eighteenth century, slaves in New York were used primarily as domestics—cleaning, cooking, and washing—held to make the lives of their enslavers easier. The gender breakdown of the population reflected this, with only 35.4 black adult males for every 100 women in 1703. Just five years before 1741, the census had the slave population of New York to be seven hundred strong, or 16.5 percent of New York's total population. By the eve of the Negro Plot, the primary purpose of slavery had changed from domestic to commercial, with slaves being trained in the trades and used to further the industry of their owners as well as their domestic needs. For additional profit, skilled and unskilled slaves were rented out to the various commercial companies that docked at Manhattan's major port. Therefore, the gender balance shifted accordingly as well, dramatically so. By 1737, the male to female ratio had sprung to 110.7 males to 100 females. By 1746, it was 126.7 to 100.

But with the increase of men came the increase in male problems. Men were more likely than women to socialize, get drunk, test the social order, and become violent. Men were also more likely to run away, or turn their frustration into armed resistance. To make matters more volatile on Manhattan isle, not only did enslaved African males significantly outnumber their female counterparts, but they also had difficulty visiting the homes of those few enslaved women that were in the colony.

With small slave holdings of mostly three slaves or less, it was unusual for couples to share a master or quarters, and many slavers took exception to nocturnal visits to their homes by their female slave's slave husband. Given the circumstance, the improbable interracial union between Caesar and Peggy makes even more sense. It wasn't as if Caesar had many women of his own race to choose from; even the ones that were around were difficult to visit privately.

The unfathomable harshness of the Africans' lives did not negate the fact that they were mortal, that they felt joy, and they felt pain, hunger, and loneliness. In the context of slavery, it was impossible for the Africans to publicly express their humanity, to live a life worth the price of it, without breaking the laws that bound them. Those laws became even tighter in 1730, when another supposed slave revolt (which was quickly proven to be a hoax) resulted in further tightening of the 1712 laws. By 1741, the slaves made up a sixth of colonial New York's population. Daniel Horsmanden accurately described the Africans as the enemies of the very households in which they lived.

Add to this equation for chaos the difficult financial straits of most of the white colonists of New York at the time. In the spring of 1741, the colony was emerging from a particularly harsh winter, which had worsened an already shaky economic condition. A long freeze meant dead crops and halted commerce. After a decade of depression, the economy of this rude little agrarian trading town had yet to move forward. While the investigation into the fires continued, so did a strike by the city's bakers, who were protesting the cost of wheat. This left a good portion of the city without bread, its staple. The city was on edge, broke and hungry.

The colony of New York was a backwater, dedicated completely to a "commercial-extractive" economy. Likewise, its citizens were largely dedicated to the pursuit of individual gain, as opposed to the building of a utopia, or other nonsense. This was not a place of high culture. Although in the past there had been occasional theater productions, from 1734 to 1750 not one play was performed in the city. Education in New York was also severely lacking. Without a satisfactory elementary school, most children either went ignorant or were home trained. Illiteracy was widespread—Mrs. Kannady, for instance, would later sign her deposition with an X—her mark. It was embarrassing; visitors to the area made note of the absence of books among these philistines. If you wanted to read a book, you had to send off to England.

This was not to say that New York didn't have ample sources of entertainment. They did, but they all involved getting drunk. Mostly these entertainments also involved animals fighting (bear-baiting, goose-pulling) to the bloody death, if the beast was unlucky, which it usually was. New Yorkers were known for being brutish and boorish, and they were so busy trying to make a buck that they didn't care.

"To talk bawdy and to have a knack att [sic] punning passes among some there for sterling wit," observed Alexander Hamilton, a barrister, transplanted from Philadelphia. Dr. Hamilton remarked on one sterling member of New York society on an occasion when that stalwart individual decided to share his personal health anecdotes with lawyer Hamilton's party, over a drink at a local pub:

"He told us he was troubled with the open piles and with that, from his breeches, pulled out a linnen [sic] hankercheff [sic] all stained with blood and showed it to the company just after we had eaten dinner."

Perhaps, the man could be forgiven. New York's health-care system was in dreadful shape, suffering from backwoods doctors with little or no training. Even those with medical training had little actual worthwhile medical knowledge. Doctored to by these quacks, the colony was virtually defenseless against the measles outbreak of 1729, and the yellow fever outbreaks in both 1732 and 1733–1735.

These, of course, were mere aftershocks compared to the

great yellow fever outbreak of 1702, which laid to waste more than 10 percent of the population. The smallpox epidemic of 1731 killed six hundred colonists, coming back for seconds in 1738. Those that the disease left alive, it left pocked and scarred, as the many runaway slave notices attest.

It was a harsh environment, populated largely by harsh people with coarse ways. Altogether, between the fear of disease and the general fear that ignorance engenders, New York's transplanted European population was on edge and ripe for pushing. The Africans among them not only had to suffer the same ills of this dysfunctional society, but they also were left to live on the lowest margin of it. The enslaved were subjugated to the will of an ignorant, insecure majority population, and dependent on these crazy white folks to be rational for their own survival.

A THING TO BE FEARED

FIRE, FIRE, MORE FIRES. And with repetition, fear. Leading to terror. Each building upon the last. Until it felt as if the island itself was ablaze.

Fear that multiplied by the day. Hogsheads of fear. So much fear that it appeared to be evidence in itself.

The logic of the colonists was simple: With this much anxiety, surely there must be a hidden cause whose evil was equal in magnitude. Clearly, there was something grand afoot. That the need for action was dire, any action, to stop it—or at least stop their anxiety of what it might be. Some gesture to calm the nerves and give back the illusion of security. Obviously, it was the Negroes—so many rumored whispers was damn near the same as incontrovertible fact. The Negroes must be conspiring, it was all but proven. But weeding them out one by one would prove a greater task. The Africans were everywhere, integrated into the fabric of the elite's daily lives. That said, there was already one known slave crime ring in custody, one that in the light of this new treachery seemed even more sinister: The African and European underclass coming to-gether could do a lot more damage to the city's social order than a few petty thefts if the culprits set their mind to it. And who was to say they hadn't already done so?

Some fires. A theft. A rowdy bar on the edge of town. Until now, these are really just separate, isolated realities, individual pieces. It should be noted: If history today links these two separate affairs—the Hogg robbery and the fires—it is be-cause in Daniel Horsmanden's account he relates them as such. Yet, peering back through time, they can also easily be seen as entirely unrelated events. In fact, if we ignore most of the colony's coerced, contemporary chorus, it makes sense that they are completely unrelated events. Horsmanden might have had reason to see them as linked even years after their occurence—to him, they were the foundation of all that was to follow. If, in fact, they were linked, Horsmanden was the great savior of his race and country. If not, he was a murderer.

Was there a plot at all? It is here, at this point in the narrative, that we must ask if this wasn't all just a horrific tale of coinci-dence and circumstance, one event piled upon another, and concocted to look connected by timing. The question must be asked now because it is at this point in the course of events that the difference between fact and fear become forever blurred, where accusation, confession, and pure terror take control.

★ ★ ★

On April 23, 1741, the informant, Mary Burton, stood before the court to continue her testimony in regard to the gang of thieves working out of Hughson's tavern. But the incident of the Hogg theft had already become a rather mundane, secondary affair to the court. While young Mary sought to continue her detailed account of the thievery, the grand jury's minds had moved on to the "burning" issue of the day. In fact, it was not what Mary said about the Hughson crime ring in her testimony that interested them and aroused their suspicion, but what she didn't say concerning the myriad arsons that were now gripping the city. What was she holding back?

That morning, when first summoned to the court, Mary sent a message via the constable that she had decided she would not be sworn in. Nor would she be giving any evidence. In response to this annoyance, the court ordered the constable to seek a summons from the magistrate to force the impetuous Burton to stand before them. When Mary finally arrived hours later, her demeanor had changed considerably since she had last come before the court. Despite the obvious gravity of her situation, she stood there, refusing to be sworn in, displaying what the judges took as "great uneasiness, or terrible apprehensions." In the many days since her last appearance, it seemed, Mary had had the opportunity to rethink her testimony.

Seeing Mary Burton's apprehension, however, did not put the grand jury in mind of the perils of being the sole witness to a significant organized crime ring. The court saw Mary's discomfort, yet it reminded them not of the task at hand, but of their own fears, their own suspicions during this anxiety-provoking time of arson. Here was a young white girl who had worked daily in the illicit lair of the Negroes, and had already admitted to being witness to their hidden guile and machinations. If there was a conspiracy among these black-skinned blackhearts (and surely there was) then Mary Burton would have been the one to see it in action. She was, after all, but a common servant girl whose presence was barely noticed by even the lowest of this society. Quickly, the judges' questions began to veer away from the theft at Hogg's, focusing on the more pressing matters at hand: What did Mary know of the fires? Was it this knowledge that had now stilled her once-jumping tongue?

To this line of inquiry, Mary Burton was silent, arousing the grand jury's suspicion even further. Her confused silence seemed to affirm their fears louder than any words could manage, so they pressed harder. But still she said nothing. Convinced now that they had found their first lead into the fires, the grand jury read to her the proclamation promising indemnity as well as one hundred pounds for any information. Such sum was *five times* what most New Yorkers could make in a year, but still Mary disdainfully refused them what they wanted so badly to hear. Threats followed. Mary Burton hadn't even opened her mouth in regard to the plague of fires, yet in the course of their one-sided inquisition the grand jury had become absolutely convinced of her knowledge of the crime. Their minds already made up, the grand jury commanded Alderman Bancker to lock up the girl for further questioning. The constable immediately took her to a cell.

To Mary Burton's credit, it was the forced march to imprisonment that broke her, not the money, nor the base need to please the powerful. The constable, given the task of escorting Mary to her cage, only made it part way, when she gave in.

Her opening act behind her, imagining full knowledge of what would happen to her if she didn't cooperate, Mary began to talk. After being brought back in front of the court and sworn in, she repeated what she knew about the burglary, about the Hughsons' involvement in the crime, along with their co-conspirators, Caesar and Prince. But what about the fires, the court asked, the burglary remaining but a prelude in their minds.

Fires?

Again Mary Burton stood silent, confused by the line of questioning. Again, the grand jury took this as concrete evidence of knowledge, or as Horsmanden put it:

"They naturally concluded, it did by construction amount to an affirmative, that she could give an account of the occasion of the several fires."

There was, of course, another way to look at Mary Burton's reaction to this inquisition: She had no idea what they were talking about. Why, for instance, would a witness who was willing to protect her own skin by testifying to the guilt of others, now arbitrarily draw a line in regard to what she would and would not disclose at the risk of her own freedom? Regardless of her motive, it would take still more and graver threats by the court, denouncements of her religious soul, entreaties that giving the confession they desired, she would not only save valuable property but the eternal souls of those who would surely lose their lives if the fires continued.

Exhausted and wanting to please, Mary Burton finally gave in.

The first article of her deposition offered nothing new: that Prince and Caesar had stolen the goods from Hogg, that the Hughsons and Peggy Kerry received them.

It was in the second article that the focus began shifting away from the original crime:

"Caesar, Prince, and Mr. Philipse's Negro man [Cuffee] used to meet frequently at my master's house," Mary testified. "And I heard them talk frequently of burning the fort. They would go down to the Fly and burn the whole town. My master and mistress said they would assist as much as they could."

With the third article of Mary Burton's deposition, we see her offer the beginning of an element that would enter into many of her depositions to come—the absurd:

"That in their common conversation they used to say, that when all this was done, Caesar should be governor, and my master, Mr. Hughson, should be king."

One can almost hear the liquor in those words if they were ever uttered, the tone of idol humor muttered in taverns everywhere.

The fourth article in her testimony, outlined by Daniel Horsmanden in his account, brought attention closer to the heart of the matter, relating to the courtroom of wealth and privilege that the lowly slave, Cuffee, often was heard to make

the point that "a great many had too much, and others too little," particularly his own master.

The fifth article provided more minor details of the theft,
Mary's last-ditch effort to appease with the details she could
reasonably deliver.

It was with the sixth, seventh, eighth, and ninth articles,
however, that Mary Burton delivered the information that the
grand jury had insisted she tell them:

6.   That at the meetings of the three aforesaid negroes,
Caesar, Prince, and Cuffee, at her master's house, they
used to say, in their conversations, that when they set fire
to the town, they would do it in the night, and as the
white people came to extinguish it, they would kill and
destroy them.

7.   That she has known at times, seven or eight guns in
her master's house, and some swords, and that she has
seen twenty or thirty negroes at one time in her master's
house; and that at such large meetings, three aforesaid
negroes, Cuffee, Prince, and Caesar, were generally present, and most active, and that they used to say, that the
other negroes durst not refuse to do what they commanded them, and they were sure that they had a number sufficient to stand by them.

8.   That her master [Hughson] and her mistress used to
threaten, that if she, the deponent, ever made mention

of the goods stolen from Mr. Hogg, they would poison her; the negroes swore, if she ever published, or discovered the design of burning the town, they would burn her whenever they met her.

9. That she never saw any white person in company when they talked of burning the town, but her master, her mistress, and Peggy.

And there it was. The outline of a revolution. Now the court had exactly what it was looking for. The Negroes were armed, scheming, lusting to rob, and murder their white captors. Serving them exactly what they asked, Mary Burton both satisfied the grand jury and left it seriously unsettled.

On the Thursday morning of April 23, the judges gathered, joined by all of the lawyers in the city. What should be done? was the question. *What should be done?* All of those present would be needed to further investigate the terror, build the case that would prosecute the guilty.

It was a crowded turnout. While the attorney general was otherwise disposed, it seemed everyone else was present, and action was soon taken. The good British and Dutch men quickly agreed that Negroes in revolt posed a heinous reality warranting their immediate attention. What struck far more nefarious about the affair for the assembled judiciary was the implication this massive plot implied. All of the men present considered themselves well acquainted with the Negro. The Negro is a passive creature by nature, created by God to serve the white man. Made by him to be naturally childlike and docile, just as he made the sheep, or cow. How is it possible? If this conspiracy existed on the level of which it had been hinted, if it was an organized thing as described, then there was no question that it must be a twisted yet brilliant white mind behind it all. It could be no other. A durst and dastardly bastard who would manipulate the childlike Negroes out of their nature and into chaos.

Now that—that there could be a white man so reckless and wrong—that was a thing to be feared indeed.

Jumping into immediate action, a gang of these judges headed to their own jail, where the one white colonist sat imprisoned who might have intimate knowledge of the Negro conspiracy. A white person connected to the evil, but not so personally responsible for it that she might be utterly unwilling to divulge its horrific truth. Standing en masse outside her cell door, the right proper gentlemen of the colony of New York stared in at the lowly whore that was Peggy Kerry, for the moment, needing something quite a deal more than what men like them would usually ask of such a woman.

"Margaret Sorubiero, this does not have to be your fate. Talk to us. There is the possibility of a pardon from the attorney general himself and the benefits of the court if you tell us what we desire to hear."

Peggy stared back at them. By this point in her life, she knew more about the nature of their desire than they did. And so she gave them nothing but her glare and denials.

Still they persisted. "Any fool can see the larger conspiracy here, Margaret Sorubiero; why not name it and begone? Who, what are you protecting? Why did you lie so easily with your persistent refusals?"

They coaxed. They bribed. They threatened. And, ultimately, they failed. Despite the dangling of amnesty, Peggy faced them, and maintained her denial of any knowledge of their imagined revolt.

"If I should accuse anybody of any such thing, I must accuse innocent persons, and wrong my own cause," she insisted. Her protests only serving to solidify her guilt in these inquisitors' minds.

Not long after, a curious note was intercepted, heading out of the city by courier. It was written in Dutch, by a female hand. Translated by the suspicious British (whose relations with the their Dutch neighbors could often be strained), it echoed conspiracy, betrayal, subterfuge. The message apparently had been meant for the recently absconded John Romme, the Dutchman, and, probably written by the wife he'd abandoned. In English it read:

Beloved Husband John Romme,

This is to acquaint you that I have received your letter by the bearer hereof and understand out of it that you intend to return home again. My dear, I desire that you make the best of your way to go further and not to come to New-York and not to make yourself known where you are for John Hughson is this day to have his tryal as also his wife, their servant maid is giving evidence against both and she has brought your name likewise in question and I am afraid John Hughson and his wife will be hanged by what I can hear and the sheriff and bailiffs seek for you every where, Vaarck's negro he keeps his word stedfast for you Brother Lucas is chosen one of the jurymen and he hears how it is.

So no more but remaining your respectful wife Elezabet Romme even till death.

Superscribed, *for Mr. John Romme,* QDG

FOR YOUR LIFE AND SOUL

THE KING AGAINST CAESAR and Prince, Negroes."
This was the introduction to the trial, but, in fact,
it wasn't actually a trial. It was a ritual. A formality. Mere
practice for what was to come. Caesar and Prince stood,
doomed. They were black, and came precondemned. The
evidence was circumstantial and hearsay but, for the likes
of these men, no more was needed. Nothing was refuted—
there was nothing they could say on their own behalf, because Africans were not even allowed to testify. The jury
was called without challenge. The theft of Hogg's merchandise repeated. The additional charge of entering the property of Abraham Meyers Cohen to rob him was added for
good measure.

If you stand as a black man in a room to be judged by white
fear and ignorance, there is no point in looking up. There is no
point in noting the words that Europeans use to sanction their
bigotry, no matter how much worth they themselves think

they are putting into them. That Mary Burton yapped to the court, or that Peggy Kerry was brought into the room only to prolong her silence, mattered little. It was an exercise. It was a play. The conclusion was already written, and no two people were more sure of that than the Africans who were meant to await their fate.

"Not guilty," the two men declared, and it would be the only words the Europeans would extract from them. Two words contradicted by the thirteen witnesses for the King, a baker's dozen who swore otherwise. Caesar and Prince had three character witnesses for their own cause, but it was just so much air, so much filler. The evidence was summed and the jury returned from their deliberation quickly. The verdict was never in question, they just removed the first word of the slaves' plea and bounced it back at them.

"Guilty!" and that was all the court needed or wanted at the moment. Guilty of theft, guilty of robbery, guilty of disposal of stolen property. There was no need yet to press the slaves for information about the fires. For slaves, robbery alone stood as capital offense. So the two men's lives were already forfeit in the eyes of the law.

The two Africans. The notorious, Caesar and Prince, now survived solely at the judges' whim, and the whites would (and could) do whatever they wanted with them. That would be to wring free of them any juicy information they had, and then dispose of them in the end like so much pulp.

★　★　★

Arthur Price was a lowlife. What random act places him in our story is that he had already gotten himself locked up for thievery. Really, the crime Price was incarcerated for was not much more resounding than were the misadventures of Hughson's rogues: A white servant of the well-respected Captain Vincent Pearse, he had been busted nicking some of the property the captain was storing for the lieutenant governor since the governor's fire. A crime of opportunity, not the kind the likes of Price could walk away from easily. And he was white, so it wasn't as if he was going to hang for his indiscretion.

Now though, Prisoner Price had seen the light. Had one of those famous jailhouse conversions. When the under-sheriff came through on his rounds, Price discreetly called him over, whispered his putrid breath into the officer's ear.

"Listen, mate, I got a story to tell. You let them judges know, good old Arthur Price has got something for them. Information. You tell them, right?"

When the under-sheriff relayed the message, the judges gave little thought to the certainty that Price's testimony was inspired by his motivation to save his own compromised hide. Or did they even consider that the opportunistic little whiner was out to get his undeniably greedy paws on the hundred-pound bounty being paid to whites with information on the fires. The judges had already made up their mind about what the truth was, so all they were looking for was confirmation. Without hesitation Arthur Price was quickly and discreetly removed from his cell and brought to the court, where after being duly sworn he gave his account.

According to Price, he had not sought the information in question. In fact, he said that Peggy Kerry came to *him* at the beginning of the last week. Right to the grate in his prison door.

" 'I'm very much afraid of those fellows telling or discovering something of me,' " he told the court Peggy had confessed to him. By "those fellows," it was clear to Arthur Price (and, certainly, the judges as well) that Peggy meant the Africans who'd been arrested. "But if they do, by God, I will hang every one of them. But, I will not forswear myself unless they bring me in."

"Peggy, how forswear yourself?" Price asked her, confused, he said, by the expression she had used.

"There is fourteen sworn," Peggy responded cryptically.

"What? Is it about Mr. Hogg's goods?"

"No, by God, about the fire," she revealed.

"Was John and his wife in it?" Price asked, fishing for the Hughsons' involvement in the matter.

"Yes, by God, they were both sworn as well as the rest."

"Are you not afraid that the Negroes would discover you?" Price said he asked Peggy.

"No," she shrugged off, "for Prince, Cuff, and Caesar, and Vaarck's Negro are all true-hearted fellows."

Eager for more, making sure he pulled from her every detail he could, knowing how priceless this information could be, Price had waited patiently for Peggy to reveal herself further. That moment came when, in reaction to her lover Caesar's trial the day before, Peggy's anxiety overwhelmed her.

After hearing for herself the damning testimony of Mary Burton, Peggy told Price, "I have no stomach to eat my victuals, for that bitch has fetched me in and made me as black as the rest about the indigo and Mr. Hogg's goods. If they do hang the two poor fellows below," Peggy said of Caesar and Prince, "the rest of the Negroes would be revenged on them yet. But if they send them away, it is another case."

Feigning support, Arthur Price offered Peggy false comfort for the wounds inflicted by Mary Burton. "I don't doubt but they will endeavor to poison this girl that has sworn."

"No, by goddamn, I don't believe that, but they will be revenged on them some other ways." It was in this moment of reflection, that Peggy noticed something amiss. Looking anew at her confidante, his desperation and eager manner, Peggy immediately questioned the wisdom of her candor.

"For your life and soul of you, you son of a bitch," she now warned Price, "don't speak a word of what I have told you."

To the assembled jury, Price related her threat as he betrayed she who had uttered it. The judges, for their part, recognized not only their course forward based on the information relayed to them, but also a new asset in their war. A traitor in the ranks of the lowly. Look at Arthur Price, standing so smug, so proud in front of them, a rat on two legs, a thief, a scallywag, one the judges could call their own. A sign that God himself was answering their prayers, delivering the tools this court needed to bring his justice into being.

★ ★ ★

Whether the conspiracy was a concrete thing of plans and machinations or simply the product of rational minds boiled in fear, the effects were starting to be seen. People believed, regardless of evidence, that the Great Negro Plot was a real threat, and this in itself brought real consequences. White people believed it. Black people believed it. At the same time Price was relating his little story, replete with line-by-line dialogue, chaos continued elsewhere. Directly across the Hudson River from New York City, in the New Jersey town of Hackensack, colonists were awoken an hour before dawn by warning calls, and arose to a scene most frightening. In the early morning darkness it appeared that no less than seven barns in the village had been set afire and were now burning in full glory. As the fires grew, so did the fear. The conspiracy loomed—it had spread across the Hudson, and now into the lands beyond. The plot was larger than could be imagined, an army of Negroes intending mass destruction.

Again, an African was seen emerging from a barn, this time with a gun in his hand.

Caught by the alarmed citizenry who were, to say the least, very conscious of the trouble of their New York neighbors on the opposite side of the river, the slave caught was recognized as a man enslaved by one Derick Van Hoorn.

"You don't understand," the slave pleaded. "I seen the man who really was responsible for the fires."

"Then what are you doing holding that rifle? Explain that away," he was pressed.

"This gun? This gun was to shoot the man what was responsible. That's what master ordered."

A sly one, the Dutch farmers concluded. Moments later, a second slave was uncovered nearby in his master's nearby house, loading a firearm of his own, two bullets in his hand ready to be placed inside. The two Africans were both arrested immediately.

The first slave captured eventually confessed to being guilty of the arson in question. The second never admitted to anything, having done nothing more than hold a gun in his hand. It didn't matter. In New Jersey, the concerned do things fast and right. Within days both had been tried, convicted, and burned alive at the stake for their crimes.

Back in Manhattan, the judges of the city could only lament that more names had not been pried out of the New Jersey Negroes before the job was done.

Arthur Price was put back to work quickly, lest his duplicitous nature be revealed before being fully exploited. Margaret Sorubiero or Salingburgh, also known as Peggy Kerry (depending on who was asking or who was spelling), had proved her nature, so now the same stimulus needed to be applied to another peripheral player. Young Sarah Hughson, daughter of John, and surely one with an ear to the occasion, was chosen as Price's next mark. A few days later, having arrived in the courthouse to witness her mother and father be formally charged, she was quickly detained and removed in bondage from the courtroom. Thrown into jail, she soon found a talkative Arthur Price conveniently occupying an adjoining cell.

From experience, knowing exactly where to take the discussion, Price started in on young Sarah, asking her pointed questions about the fires to see her response. The answers she gave at first were indirect, yet weighted.

"I went to a fortune teller," she told the man caged beside her, "who told me that in less than five weeks' time I would come to trouble if I did not take good care of myself." It certainly seemed a bleak fortune that had already appeared to have come true. "But after that I will come to good fortune," Sarah assured the informant.

"What of your father's fortune?" Price egged her on.

"My father will be tried and condemned, but not hanged. He is to go over the water," she said.

Price had Sarah where he wanted her. Prodding her forward, masking his way to appear meandering and casual when it was in fact altogether direct and focused, he finally got to the subject of the rebellion, opening the door by telling Sarah that some of the slaves involved had been discovered and had already started talking.

"I know nothing of any plot," Sarah responded definitively.

"They that were sworn in the plot had discovered and brought them every one in." Arthur Price lied to the teenager, the effects of the lie visible immediately, as Sarah blushed at the thought of it. As she nervously replaced her bonnet back on her head in a tell of her true desire to hide from him and the revelation, Sarah's cheeks lost their red as her face went flush, and then she blushed ruddy all over again.

"Do you know who it was? What have you heard?" Sarah asked him.

"Oh, I heard it by and by, and it was kept private," Price told her, insinuating an intimate involvement and trustworthy nature when in fact he possessed neither.

Sarah was frozen. Her mind moving, adjusting to this knowledge of her most primal fears for her fate. It was a long moment before she could gather enough composure to speak. "It must be either Holt's Negro, or Todd's," she said, thinking out loud, "for we were always afraid of them and mistrusted them, though they were as bad as the rest and were to have set their own masters' houses on fire. I wish that Todd had sent his black dog away, or sold him, when he was going to do it." This last little detail only adding to the credibility of Mr. Arthur Price's later recantation of the conversation when it was discovered by the investigating judges that Mr. Todd had *indeed* intended to get rid of his slave, as was the custom with unruly human merchandise.

"You had better tell everything you know," Price pressed her, "for that may be of some service to your father."

"No," Sarah insisted, "for they are doing all they can to take his life away. I would sooner suffer death and be hanged with my daddy if he is to be hanged, than give them that satisfaction of telling or discovering anything to them."

Despite the duplicitous Price's pleading, Sarah was determined, as much as she was despondent.

"I should have gone into the country," she lamented. "Like a fool that I was I did not go up in the country! I stayed to see what would happen to my mama and daddy, but now I would go. I'll be hanged if ever they should get me in York again." Gone now was the casual optimism of only moments before. Only fear and anger seemed to remain. And bitterness. Thinking of the city and its denizens that had now become her persecutors, Sarah had only threats to offer:

"If they had not better care for themselves, they will have a great deal more damage and danger in York than they are aware of," she warned. "If they do hang my daddy, they better do something else." Adding knowingly, "As for the fire at the fort, they did not set the saddle on the right horse."

The last cryptic comment, Arthur Price explained to the assembled jury at the end of his tale, meant that the judges had yet to look in the right direction for the real mastermind behind the fire at the fort.

Of the other Africans mentioned by Sarah, Mr. Holt, a local dancing instructor, already had the foresight to remove his slave from the city, thereby avoiding losing his costly personal property to a court that very well might decide to destroy it. Dundee, Mr. Todd's slave, was less fortunate, and was taken up immediately.

Peggy Kerry must have sensed Arthur Price's deceit soon after allowing her tongue to slip in his presence, having spent a life around characters of his order. Seeing him back in his old cell, she hissed through the bars, "Do not discover anything for your life, for if you do, by God, I will cut your throat."

But despite her brittle bravado, momentum had continued to gain on Peggy Kerry, and soon it would be she herself speaking to the judges directly, beseeching them, making compromises to appease a court whose hunger had yet to find boundaries, bartering with the truth to save her own skin and the skins of the people she loved above all else.

THEY DIED VERY STUBBORNLY

B Y THE TIME PEGGY, alleged prostitute and known companion of Negroes, stepped forward with a confession of her own, she held little doubt that Arthur Price, the accused thief, was already doing enough talking for the both of them. If Peggy was to save her own life, she knew, she must turn storyteller herself, regardless of either past oaths or lack of knowledge. Reaching out to the court before Price could offer any more damning testimony on her behalf, Peggy volunteered the following statement for dictation by the jail secretary:

> That I was several times at the house of John Romme, shoe-maker, and tavern-keeper, and saw several meetings of the negroes from time to time; and in particular, in the month of December last past, I saw assembled there in or about ten or twelve in number, vz.—Cuff, belonging to Mr. Philipse; Brash, Mr. Jay's; Curacao Dick, a negro man; Caesar, Pintard's; Patrick, English's; a negro belonging to Mr. Breasted in Pearl-street, (Jack) Cato, Alderman Moore's.

The rest of the names that were in the combination, I cannot remember, of their master's names. They proposed, to burn the fort first, and afterwards the city; and then steal, rob and carry away all the money and goods they could procure, and was to be carried to Romme's and were to be joined by the country negroes; and that they were to murder every one that had money.

The reason why I did not make this discovery before, Romme swore them all never to discover, and swore me too; and I thought, I would wrong my own soul, if discovered it. And that all the rest of the negroes in city and country were to meet in one night.

All the above I am ready to declare upon oath.

This admission Peggy signed with an X, the mark of an illiterate. It was sent to the judges from jail so that those on the bench could see that the stubborn woman had begun to see the error in her ways. The conviction of Prince, and the one who claimed her love, Caesar, had jarred her mind. Peggy Kerry (or Keary or Sarinbirr, as this document variously declared her) was now telling the truth of the matter, giving herself over to the will of the court.

The judges seemed to believe that she was moving in the right direction with her new testimony, in the direction of what they wanted to hear, but when looking at this confession, with a basic knowledge of her situation, the subtractions prove most daring. While Peggy pointed her finger at many, it was those omitted from her statement that say the most about her state of mind. Most obvious is the complete absence of the Hughsons from the plot. Peggy moved the scene of the crime away from Hughson's tavern to Romme's, removing the name Hughson from the story altogether. It was clever, and so much safer. John Romme was on the run, elusive and comparatively untouchable, while John Hughson, along with wife and daughter, was in custody and facing execution. As was Peggy. Yet, even more important, the Hughsons' extended family was currently holding Peggy's son for safekeeping. How could she possibly say anything to incriminate them?

Even more interesting is the list of the slaves named in the conspiracy: The first mentioned was Caesar. But while Peggy had denied her relationship to her Caesar, who was the legal property of the Vaarck family, in attempt to throw off the judges, she had replaced him with another slave with the same name, *Pintard's* Caesar. The judges could barely keep the slaves straight already—even with the list in front of them, the court tripped over itself when the city constables brought in English's Cork instead of Patrick's Cork. (Patrick's Cork giving such an impressively innocuous, "happy darky" performance that he was released immediately.) Peggy's confession was a ploy—by her, to add to the confusion—with full knowledge of her lover's conviction; it was very well an attempt to exonerate *her* Caesar through reduction.

But if Peggy's deposition was an attempt to free Caesar from the grip of this court, it was a failed one. Regretfully, nothing was going to save this man in this world now. The next day, Friday, May 8, 1741, the second of the court's three justices began reading his decision in the case of the two slaves, Caesar and Prince, convicted of capital crimes:

"I have great reason to believe that the crimes you now stand convicted of, are not the least of those you have been concerned in, for by your general characters you have been very wicked fellows, hardened sinners, and ripe, as well as ready, for the most enormous and daring enterprises," the court's only regret being that the man could not be convicted of more.

"Especially you, Caesar," the judge castigated, pausing to single out and address individually the insolent beast. "And as the time you have yet to live is to be but very short, I earnestly advise and exhort both of you to employ it in the most diligent and best manner you can, by confessing your sins, repenting sincerely of them, and praying God in his infinite goodness to have mercy on your soul."

It was the ultimate hypocrisy: men who had been robbed of their very lives being convicted of theft by the people who'd taken everything from them.

Mercy, it seems, was not to be the concern of the court, nor its intention. After further entreaties to Caesar and Prince to speak of their fellow slaves, it was declared that the two were to be taken from their jail to the place of their execution. The hanging, by the neck until dead, for the burglary of Hogg's store, would be carried out on the following Monday morning. It was further ordered that the body of the rascal Caesar, then be removed from the noose and hung in chains in the square. A message to all slaves and their illicit overseers of the fate that could await them.

After the sentencing, the judges gathered to discuss the confession received from Peggy Kerry via the jailer the night before. The shifting of the scene of the crime from Hughson's to Romme's had been missed by no one, and no one was amused.

Peggy Kerry was brought to stand in front of the bench.

"Do you understand the seriousness of this matter? That to testify against innocent persons is a grave crime in itself?" the justices harangued her.

The latter would become a particularly interesting question considering what the court had asked (and would ask) of Mary Burton.

Peggy looked on evenly at her inquisitors.

"I certainly do," she responded, knowing it a very serious matter indeed. She was more intimate certainly with what was at stake than they were.

Regardless, it seemed to the judges that if the "Irish beauty" was not at the moment telling the complete truth of the matter, she was, in part, leading up to doing it. Or, at least, toward the direction they would see the truth go.

The court assembled the next day to hear a more detailed account of Peggy's version of events. By this time, she already knew the fate of her enslaved lover, that he had been condemned to hang for his crime. Her attempt to exonerate him had failed, but to her mind the battle was not over. The pressure was now on Peggy to save herself, to give the story that would let her escape from this witch hunt with all that was left her, her life.

Officially recorded, this time with the name of her past marriage, Salingburgh, the woman born Margaret Kerry was now prepared to tell the best kind of tale. The kind laced with specific facts. Those accurate, little details that can afford fiction a sense of reality.

Peggy attested she moved in with Frank, a free Negro, the fall before. As a woman fallen from marriage, she admitted, she was not very picky, and his lodgings along the new Battery suited her fine. Over time, Peggy became aware of one of her neighbors, a local shoemaker that lived three or four doors down from her new residence. That man was John Romme. Peggy told the court, she quickly noticed Romme was an odd fellow. For one thing, it seemed there was many a Negro coming to and fro his house. Or rather, they staggered to and fro, as they were usually blind drunk on drams, reeking of punch and other strong liquors. Romme kept a public house, one that openly served a Negro clientele. Not that Peggy was looking for such trouble, but it was impossible to ignore. It was a common thing for the Romme house to be wide awake until two, even three, in the morning, as singing was heard, cups filled, and dice rolled freely.

That the house was one of the many that flagrantly ignored the colony's moral codes was common knowledge. But the level of illicit behavior revealed itself to Peggy that November.

It was on a Sunday evening between the night hours of eleven P.M. and twelve A.M. that Peggy saw the suspicious sight of two Negroes passing through the darkness, each carrying the considerable weight of a firkin of butter on their muscular shoulders. Why in the dark? she had wondered, for there was definitely something suspicious about the scene. Peggy was sure she was witnessing a crime, and ducked into the shadows of the nearby shed of Mr. Hunt's to bear witness. The darkness was full and thorough, making it too dark to identify the Africans, whose dark skin further obscured their features. Pausing though, muting her breath so she did not reveal herself, Peggy waited long enough to see the men leave *sixteen* of the weighted barrels inside Romme's gate.

The court listened, patiently. All this, of course, was still on the subject of petty crime, but what Peggy was doing was merely setting the scene, the context of John Romme as a ringleader of thieving slaves, so that her next revelations fit that much more into context.

It was one evening about Christmastime, just months ago, she went on, when at about eight or nine o'clock, she was socializing at the house of John Romme. A friendly neighborly congregation, nothing more, she said. Suddenly, the door flew open and in walked ten or twelve Negroes, come to make merry. Clearly far more people than the law allowed in such establishment, but Romme was turning no man away.

"Look how well the rich people in this place lived," Peggy said Romme observed to the Africans as each grabbed his own mug and aimed to make the better of it. "If you would be advised by me, we should have the money," Romme, she said, continued.

"How wilt you manage that?" Cuffee, Mr. Philipse's legal property, replied.

"Well enough," said Romme. "Set them all a light fire. Burn the houses of them that have the most money, and kill them all, as the Negroes would have done their masters and mistresses formerly."

Not lost on the Africans, Romme was making a direct reference to the revolt of 1712, still present and immediate in all their minds.

"I will be captain over you till you can get all their money, and then I would be governor." How many drinks might have gone down Romme's gullet before this came out, Peggy did not bother to recall.

Nor if there was a smile to go along with this absurdity.

Cuffee, she said, dismissed Romme's grand scheming. " We could not do it," she said her lover said.

"Yes! We'll do well enough," Romme countered. "We'll send into the country for the rest of the Negroes to help, because I can write, and I know several Negroes in the country who can read. You can do it, and I will stand by you. The sun will shine very bright by and by, and never fear, my lads." Romme continued with his assurances. "But if it should happen that anything should come out, I will make my escape to North Carolina, Cape Fear, or somewhere thereabouts. Or into the Mohawk's country, where I lived before. But besides, the Devil cannot hurt me, for I have a great many friends in town, and the best place would stand for me."

The plan, according to Romme, was simple. "Burn the fort first, and afterwards the city, and then steal and rob, and carry away all the money and goods you can procure. It should be brought to my house, and I will take care to hide it.

"If the fire does not succeed, and we can not compass our ends that way, then I propose to you that you should steal all you can from your masters, for I would carry you to a strange country and give you your liberty, and set you free. That is whether you like my proposal."

"There's great talking, and no cider," Cuffee complained, at which time the revelries ended. The plan's attractiveness appeared only as strong as the drink that fueled it. Romme, cautious that the treason might be reported, then forced the whole lot of the Negroes to swear to secrecy. Not even Peggy was exempt, and her silence was sworn on her immortal soul, as she was then forced to kiss a book.

"Although I know not whether or not it was a Bible," Peggy, the illiterate, reluctantly admitted to the court.

That there was a dialogue going on among prisoners about the events of the outside world is evident from this little tale. It is not mere coincidence that immediately after the attempted rebellion in Hackensack, Peggy's story adjusted to encompass an uprising spreading beyond New York's village. Peggy's knowledge of Romme's absconding, and probably the spy mentioned to the court in the translated letter of Romme's wife, is referenced also, with Peggy being so kind as to attempt to send the search for Romme on a wild-goose chase into Mohawk country.

Peggy was also generous enough to the court to add more names for them to digest. Besides Cuffee there was now Curaçao Dick, Pintard's Caesar, Weaver's Will, and Mr. Moore's Cato. "The Devil take the failer," Peggy said Cuffee had warned the group on departure. It was a message of which many of these men would have been reminded when the constables arrived to drag them off to jail. Now Peggy knew that she herself had been taken into the Devil's care as well.

Elizabeth Romme was immediately interviewed in regard to Peggy's accusations. It was a difficult position that she was in. How much could she say to protect herself without dooming her spouse? So Elizabeth, of course, started by denying everything—the specifics, the context, the general idea. Within her denials, though, Mrs. Romme did make room for other facts, as given.

"Well, yes, there had been some firkins of butter, that much is true, but as to the nature of them I have no knowledge," insisted Elizabeth Romme. "My husband conducted the business."

"This is all you know, you are swearing here under oath?" prodded the judges.

"Well, I must confess that Cuffee's father did on occasion store game fowls at our house. And brought the victuals. And sticks of wood during the long winter. And, yes, the Negroes did come to our home to drink drams on a few occasions, but rarely more than past the legal limit of three. And rarely that many."

Elizabeth added, "But when there were three, it was usually the same group of characters. Cuffee, but also Prince, and Vaarck's Caesar, who was a regular customer," correcting the biggest omission from Peggy's earlier testimony, and thereby placing Peggy's Caesar back in the center of it all.

The jail was brimming, veritably overflowing with Negroes. Yet, they would have to make room for more on the way. The newest and most important slave to become resident, aside from the two who had already been convicted and sentenced to death, was Philipse's Cuffee. The judges already had their secret weapon, and with the new focus on Cuffee they were quick to use it. Arthur Price was dispatched to do his magic again.

Cuffee didn't know Arthur Price was a traitor. To Cuffee, Price was just another white, lowlife character, recognizable from the underworld of this little village. Cuffee had not prepared himself, he was not on guard. He was just scared and bored and lonely. So Cuffee talked to the man.

"Why is Peggy called down so often?" Cuffee nervously observed to Price. It must have seemed considerably suspicious to him, particularly as he was made to sit and wait for days on end to be formally brought before the court for the first time. Not helping matters was Peggy's manner toward him. She should be forgiven in this respect, however. After all, she was the one who'd implicated him in the first place.

"I think she is discovering the plot about the fire," Price confirmed for him.

"She can not do that unless she forswears herself. I know, for he that had done that was sworn after she was in prison. I left my master's house in the evening and went along the wharves to the Fly Market, and waited there till one Quack came out of his master's house. We went to the house of John Hughson, where we met nobody but Hughson, his wife, and daughter Sarah. We called for a tankard of punch, and Hughson swore Quack three times."

"I believe I know this Quack," Price bluffed. "He lives with a butcher."

"No, he doth not live with a butcher, he lives with a painter who lives within a few doors of a butcher," Cuffee told him, unaware he was being manipulated by Price. "Quack is married to a Negro woman who is cook to the fort. To the governor, as I understand."

"How did Quack do it?"

"I don't know how he did it, but that Quack was to do it, and did do it," Cuffee insisted.

"Do you not think that the firing will be found out?" Price asked.

"No, by God, I do not think it ever will."

"Are you not afraid that the two Negroes who are to be executed Monday would discover?"

Cuffee remained confident of Caesar and Prince's integrity. "I am not afraid of that, for I'm sure that they will be burnt to ashes before they will discover it. I would lay my life on it," Cuffee continued. But, of course, he already had.

Still, lingering on the situation, Cuffee could make no sense of it. Looking around at the jail told him immediately who had been captured, and who remained free.

"I wonder why they only took up the Long Bridge Boys and did not take up those of the Smith's Fly? For I believe, if the truth was known, they are as much concerned as we."

An intriguing statement, the judges thought later when Arthur Price eagerly recanted it. The Smith's Fly Boys, referencing the slave men living in the affluent quarters of the Smith's Fly neighborhood near Pearl Street. There were two major neighborhoods where affluent colonists lived with slaves, one on the east side and one on the west. Each had its own gang of slave compatriots, now seemingly complicit. Based on this information, one of the Smith's Fly Boys, Roosevelt's Quack (not to be confused with Walter's Quack, the already incarcerated slave who had uttered the line "Fire, fire") was apprehended.

On Monday, May 11, the "very wicked fellows," Caesar and Prince, were escorted out to the gallows in accordance with their sentence. They knew they were going to die. This knowledge had been with them for a few weeks now. They also were fully aware their deaths was going to be painful, and that it wouldn't be suffocation that killed them, but the weight of their own bodies being launched down from the hangman's noose, snapping their necks. They knew that their bowels would empty into their pants, but that they wouldn't smell it. Because they'd be dead.

They knew all that, and yet they were defiant. Caesar and Prince, two African men whose powerful names were a joke on their complete lack of power. They knew, also, that regardless of any petty criminal actions they may have taken in comparison to their purported victims they were, in actuality, the righteous ones. So, despite the continued inquisition, in the face of the very people who had damned them, they remained adamantly silent.

"Who else is involved in this horrendous action?"

Nothing.

"Who was your master in these despicable acts?"

Not a word.

Caesar and Prince died honorably, naming no one, condemning no others, either out of fear, or out of concern for their already doomed hides. They proved Cuffee right; there was no discovery here. The only thing Caesar had confessed to, in the end, was his relationship with Peggy Kerry. And while Peggy never admitted that she loved him, too, she showed it by trying to omit him from all crimes she reported. This she did at her own peril.

The Africans died very stubbornly, Horsmanden wrote, refusing to confess to the last breath. Then, after all breathing was behind them, the body of Caesar was removed from the gibbet. Shoved into an iron cage, it was then rehung by the powder house as a warning to all the other slaves of what might very well befall them.

In the end, the judges didn't need Caesar or Prince to talk. The sight of the once notorious enslaved, Caesar, proud and defiant, rotting perpetually before their eyes through the weeks ahead, would open more than enough mouths on its own.

For others, it was the smell that did it.

"GOD DAMN ALL THE
WHITE PEOPLE"

JOHN ROMME HAD NOT RUN OFF into the bush of
Cape Fear to lose himself in the humid southern swamp.
Neither had he scurried off into Mohawk country seeking
asylum amongst the natives, busily rubbing mud into his face
to hide his pinkness from the world. Nor had Romme left
the country for some unnamed tropical island with a cache
of Negroes in tow, ready, as promised, to start the great slave
rebellion. No, none of that for John Romme. As it turned
out, he had remained a bit closer. John Romme was in New
Jersey.

There a magistrate encountered him, identified the hapless
shoemaker, and seized him for the New York authorities.
Within a few days Romme was back in Manhattan, stewing in
a jail cell. The "mastermind" was brought before the court to
meet the charges against him. Standing in front of the judges,
he hardly seemed the criminal genius of the paranoid imagination. Still, knowing how serious the case had become, Romme
made no attempt to deny he was some kind of criminal.

"In regards to these accusations, I only agree to knowledge of the firkins of butter, as they were brought forth to mine house by Negroes," Romme admitted.

"So you admit freely then, as your goodly wife, Elizabeth, testified before this court before, that you received said stolen goods from these Negroes?"

"Me?" John Romme responded out of a cloud of faux confusion. "She said that *I* was the one to receive the firkins? Oh, no, sir, there seems to be an error. It was not I, not I at all."

The judges paused and looked up, caught off guard by this unexpected last-minute turn.

"It was not you, you say? Well then, who do you say received these thieving Negroes?"

"Well . . ." Romme paused, almost sheepishly. "My wife, sirs. I quite innocently, I assure you, knew absolutely nothing of the matter."

In hopes of clearing matters, his wife, Elizabeth, was brought back to court for further questioning, and it soon became fairly obvious to her the gist of her husband's testimony.

Later, when Elizabeth Romme passed her husband in his cell on return to her own, John stuck his head out of the wicket to greet her.

"My darling, alas, we are reu—"

Smack!

Elizabeth "civilly saluted him with a smart slap on the chops," Horsmanden later gleefully reported.

Peggy Kerry's only hope now was to keep talking. With Caesar, her lover, already executed for his crimes (real and imagined), she saw no reason to hold back.

"It was Caesar, the Negro who I'd seen, who stole the firkins of butter," Peggy now proclaimed.

After all, there was no more damage they could to him now. His rotting corpse, hanging mere yards from the courthouse, gave testament to that fact.

"Truth be known, 'twas a week before that I did hear John Romme planning the deal with Caesar, directing the slave to the site of the butter, haggling over the cost per firkin."

"Are you certain, Peggy Kerry, that on this day you tell the whole truth?"

" 'Tis the truth. True sworn," Peggy responded immediately to the judge. Pointing across the courtroom at John Romme, she said, "Caesar had stolen for Romme that very overcoat that he wears. He took it off a boat in the docks along with some cash he gave to Romme to cover his drinking tab."

In unison the crowded room all turned to have a gawk at the coat in question, while John Romme did his best to sink his head and disappear within it.

★ ★ ★

News of Mary Burton's gossip made for quick and easy gossip itself. Just a day or two after her first examination by the grand jury, acid tongues were already busy on the cobbled streets of New York. The sole person remaining free from her former circle, Mary was casually walking past Mr. Vaarck's door. There, at this home of the late Caesar, another of Vaarck's slaves, the boy, Bastian, and the enslaved, called Tom Peal, loitered.

"Have you discovered anything more about the fires?" Peal taunted Mary as she passed.

"No," Mary quickly answered.

"Damn you," Bastian threatened, "it is not best for you, for fear you should be burnt next."

This, Mary Burton told the court at yet another deposition, after which she went on to identify a number of additional slaves she claimed had been past visitors to Hughson's tavern, including Quack. Mary Burton was indeed learning how to please these powerful men who gave her so many compliments, gifts of ducats, and promises of freedom. On this day what they needed from her was a connection of Hughson with Romme, to make sense of the contradicting story recently given.

"The two men would often retire together, off to a room alone, talking secretively in Dutch," she complied. "'Tis true, though I was not to hear it. Romme himself would sometimes tell Hughson that he feared my hearing."

"You need not be afraid of her," Romme responded,

according to Mary, "for she is bound to me and dare not tell, for if she did I would murder her."

The court would soon find yet another teenager whose mouth, once pried open, stayed open. This time, unlike Mary, the compliant one was male and a slave, which gave Sandy (also known as Sawney) even greater credence when addressing the court and speaking of the center of the conspiracy. In Sandy, the judges had another child eager to do their bidding, someone they had no trouble manipulating to their own ends.

Sandy came to the court's attention through another, having been implicated by a young slave of Mrs. Carpenter who had come on his own to the authorities to report that Sarah, the slave wench of the Niblet household, had confided in him that Sandy was involved in the fire at the fort, as well as the fire next to his master's house and the one at Alderman Bancker's. This Sarah, when brought in front of the court said, as she trembled violently in terror, that she, too, was committed to the plot, despite her initial denials.

Sandy's owner claimed the suspect boy was in Albany, then pleaded, "I know no harm of him." Sensing his expensive human property was in jeopardy of being seized and, perhaps, even destroyed, Mr. Niblet reluctantly complied, and the enslaved boy was returned to the city, and brought in to court a week later.

Knowing his terror would make him pliable, the court let

young Sandy simmer for a week in the putrid conditions of the jail, soaking in the sheer fear of so many others, before even bothering to talk to him. Still, despite the stultifying experience, Sandy came forth with nothing more than denials. He knew nothing, he claimed. He did nothing.

"I was involved in no way," he insisted.

The judges instructed him to tell the truth, and he did, but it was not the truth they wanted to hear. So he was sent back to his cell again. For one . . . two . . . seven more days. Letting the reality of his situation become even more forboding, the wants and desires of the court to become his wants and desires. After which, when a worn and exhausted Sandy stood before the judiciary once more, he still stuck by the same denials.

The judges, utterly single minded, decided it was because fear still held his tongue.

"Young man, you have no fear with cause, and no foul swear can truly bind you. You will be pardoned in the eyes of this court and God if you simply tell them the truth," he was told. But young as he was Sandy was smart enough not to take the hollow word of the judges for granted.

"The time before, when the Negroes told all they knew, then the white people hanged them," Sandy replied. The ghost of 1712 hung thick in the room. The judges knew to what he referred, and expressed outrage and indignation.

"These 1712 confessors whom you reference were merely pardoned and sent off," he was lectured, the judges either lying outright, or deliberately ignorant to the whole truth.

Finally, Sandy, knowing his predicament, knowing he was trapped, decided to give the court what they wanted. A confession tailored to keep these madmen at bay.

About three weeks before the fort fire, Sandy told the court, he was approached by Quaco (as he knew Quack) on the street. "The fort—I will see it burnt," the older slave purportedly said. "But it is a big job and you must help me."

Sandy said he responded no. "I would not run the risk of being hanged," he explained, "but I might go to hell and be damned."

Later, joining the discussion, Cuffee made his own intentions known to Sandy as well.

" 'We shall burn Philipse's storehouses to the ground. Damn him, that hang me or burn me, I will set fire to the town,' " Sandy said Cuffee told him.

To hear Sandy tell it, these were not the only two people at the ready for an arsonists' rebellion. According to him, there was a legion eager to start their own fires as well: Curaçao Dick, Bosch's Francis, Gomez's Cuffee, English's Patrick, Moore's Cato. Sandy's recitation of names went on, in all listing fourteen slaves and their specific arson projects. Four of his accused were Spanish Negroes. Sandy even had Captain Lush's William declaring, "If they do not send me over to my own country, I will ruin the city."

But this performance, for Sandy, was but a warm-up. Back in the cage for another three days, Sandy had even more to offer. The Philadelphia Quakers were right: It was amazing what solitary confinement could do for the soul.

After his slight respite, brought back in front of the court, Sandy continued his testimony. Going by Comfort's one Sunday night a month before the fires began, he said, he felt a tug on his arm from the shadows. Suddenly, Sandy swore, he found himself in a room packed with twenty of his fellow enslaved.

"Have a drink, you lad," he said he was encouraged. And once he pulled a dram to his lips, someone said, "We want you to burn some houses."

Stunned by the request and not prepared with an answer, Sandy alleged he stood speechless.

"Damn you if you refuse your task," Burk's Sarah swore at him.

Others joined in, some pulling out their rusty knifes and threatening him.

"You're to burn the Slip Market, boy. They'll be no refusing. Now swear the oath, as we have all done."

A book was brought forth, and Sandy's brown hand forced on to it.

"May God Almighty strike us dead with the first thunder if we betray one this plot." They swore, and the oath, according to Sandy, was meant literally.

The only thing Sandy didn't help the court with was the location, having never been to either Hughson's or Romme's. To make up for his shortcoming, he offered up Machado's Diana, instead, who he placed setting fire to the shingles of her master's roof.

"She's a mad one," Sandy insisted. "Her hatred is so that

she had before taken her nursing baby from her breast and purposely laid it in the cold to die rather than let it come to her master."

Based on this fourteen-year-old's allegations, four more slaves were rounded up, including Sarah, Burke's enslaved, whom he testified cursed him. This, Sarah denied, along with all involvement.

Sandy was placed before her in hope of loosening her tongue, in order to show her the resolve and resources of the judges.

"Do you deny having contact with this boy?" questioned the prosecutor.

"Indeed I did, down by the water pump, where he talked to me recently."

"What did he say, Sarah?"

"Sandy said, 'God damn all the white people, for if I had it in my power, I would set them all on fire.'" Saying this Sarah looked right at Sandy, extracting from him what she knew would be her own bit of revenge.

With all this happening in such quick order, it seemed as if the only person not talking anymore was the low thief, Arthur Price.

But that was only because he had run out of people to squeal on. The last bit of information Price would deliver to the court was that Cuffee, the Long Bridge Boy, sat in his jail cell, reading sometimes, waiting for the inevitable.

"I know I am to suffer death," Price said Cuffee lamented. "I wonder why they have not brung me to my trial, for I am sure I am to go the same way the other two went."

Shortly after that, according to Price, Quack was brought in. Cuffee saw him and he knew. As his blood began to drain and his bowels boil, he must have finally realized. Looking at the Smith's Fly Boy limp past him to his cell, Cuffee undoubtedly realized it had been his own comments to Arthur Price that had been the cause of Quack's arrest.

Cuffee never mentioned again anything of the fires to Price. The only thing Arthur Price heard from Cuffee after that, he attested, was the frequent sound of Cuffee's sobbing.

THE MONSTROUS INGRATITUDE
OF THIS BLACK TRIBE

CUFFEE AND QUACK WERE ESCORTED into court together.

Cuffee knew he had no hope. Quack knew he would fare no better.

"May it please your honours," the prosecutor began, "Gentlemen of the jury, this is a cause of very great expectations, it being, as I conceive, a matter of the utmost importance that ever yet came to be tried in this province. *Gentlemen*, there is a conspiracy of black and whites, and these two are at the center of it. They met at John Hughson's. Quack's own confessions to others proves his guilt. Cuffee is no better."

Cuffee, who was Kofi. Quack, who was Quaco, sometimes referred to as Kwaku, sealed together for eternity. The court was trying the enslaved two at a time, because it was more expedient that way.

"*Gentlemen*, it is in you, the people, in general, place their hopes and expectations of their future security and repose;

that they may sit securely in their own houses, and rest quietly in their beds, no one daring to make them afraid."

After all that waiting, Cuffee would have his day in court, perhaps, in the end, sooner than he might have wanted. Witnesses were called. Arthur Price retold his tale of Cuffee's jail-house banter, Sarah Higgins testified she had seen Cuffee in his blue coat lurking behind Philipse's storehouse with three others before fire broke out. John Peterson placed Cuffee at the site of the fire right when it erupted, having handed him a bucket himself, despite Adolph Philipse's assertion that his slave was elsewhere working. Isaac Gardner took it further, saying Cuffee joined in the bucket brigade only to dump the water on the ground as he laughed with the other slaves, the firm dirt around him turning to mud. Jacobus Stoudenburg retold his roof sighting of the slave running from the scene of the crime, Cuffee's escape only slowed by a nail that caught his breeches.

Of course, the day's events would not be complete without some words spoken by Mary Burton, she, who by this time, had become the veritable foundation on which the whole of the case laid. Not to be outdone, Mary arrived with something new to offer the court in addition to her past testimony.

"Three weeks after I arrived at Hughson's," she said, "about midwinter's last, the Negroes were there talking of the plot." The gathered crowd that filled the courtroom hushed to hear the latest of the young woman's revelations. "Some of them said perhaps I would tell, and Cuffee said, 'No, she will not, for I intend to have her for a wife!' Then he ran up to me, and I had a dishclout in my hand, which I dabbed in his face, and he ran away."

The full room emitted a collective gasp at the sexual outrage of it. The sheer audacity!

By law, slaves were allowed to give testimony only against other slaves—not white people—and this was explained to the court before Sandy was brought forth to attest to Cuffee's bragging of the intended act of burning the storehouse. Then came another slave, Fortune, stepping forward to recount his story of Quack's dragging him to the fort with the false promise of punch, and his gloating afterward that the fort had been turned into cinders.

" 'Don't you remember what I told you, there would be great alterations in the fort?' " Fortune said Quack had reminded him, and this recounted utterance, the seeming realization of personal vengeance and power, now served only to reduce Quack further.

Witnesses were called for the defense—white slave owners who had the respect of the court—but their testimony proved weak and awkward. The most damaging of which for Cuffee would come from his own master, the prominent Adolph Philipse himself, who was feeling particularly uncomfortable with the position considering the politicized nature of the court (as well as the fact that one of the judges in the case, Judge Philipse, was his own nephew). Adolph stated only that he had left Cuffee sewing a vane aboard his boat, adding damningly, "As to his character I can say nothing."

For Quack, the final blow would be delivered by John McDonald, a soldier at the fort who on the day of the fire had stood sentry at the gate.

McDonald was sitting at his post as usual, he said. The fort itself was relatively empty, what with the troops off in the Caribbean fighting the Spaniards. Quack had come up to the gate, and asked to come in. This, in itself, was not much of a surprise, Quack's wife was the lieutenant governor's cook, and this was the only way he could see her. But that was precisely why her employer didn't want him coming in; Quack was distracting his help. In fact, the last time he tried to get in, McDonald testified he had had to push Quack down to the ground to keep him from shoving past, and the guard had ended up with a punch in the face from the slave for his efforts. After all that, the slave had run to the kitchen anyway. So on the morning of the fire, it had been time for a different approach.

"The lieutenant governor has for some time forbid you from coming to the fort," McDonald said he had informed him.

"I am free now and have liberty to come," Quack answered. So the soldier, not wanting to be bothered with drama that he didn't really care about in the first place, just let Quack pass into the fort despite his order.

When McDonald spoke as much to the court, nothing was

said about why Quack ran to find refuge in the kitchen after the ruckus had begun. No mention was made of the fact that Quack was not in actuality trying to storm the fort, but *visit his wife*. This was an investigation into neither the source nor the validity of the man's anger.

"Gentlemen," the prosecutor beseeched the court. "The monstrous ingratitude of this black tribe is what exceedingly aggravates their guilt. Their slavery among us is generally softened with great indulgence. They live without care, and are commonly better fed and clothed and put to less labour than the poor of most Christian countries."

Within the paradigm of the English language there are some acknowledged great words: Hypocrisy. Gall. Delusion. Perversion. Grotesquery.

Really, one can choose from any number of these words to give character to the views that were spewed on the part of the court that day. From a distance of centuries, however, their absurdity is overwhelming, breathtaking. What similar comments made by our own contemporary courts, politicians, and leaders of industry will strike similarly putrid chords centuries down the line? What will revolt our descendants as much as this bile meant to justify one of the greatest acts of inhumanity of the millennia?

"They are indeed slaves, but under the protection of the law, none can hurt them with impunity," the judge declared, as he and the court did just that. "They are really more happy in this place than in the midst of the continual plunder, cruelty, and rapine of their native countries. But notwithstanding all the kindness and tenderness with which they have been treated amongst us, yet this is the second attempt of the same kind, that this brutish and bloody species of mankind have made within one age."

The whites were indignant, generally confused. How could these black bastards be so ungrateful after all that had been done for them?

There were some things the jury would have no trouble deciding. They were out for mere minutes.

"You both now stand convicted of one of the most horrid and detestable pieces of villainy that ever Satan instilled into the heart of human creatures to put in practice," the third of the three judges took the initiative to address the now convicted. He was brimming with indignation at the Africans' lack of appreciation for the benevolence of their people's kidnapping, rape, and life imprisonment.

"Ye that were for destroying us without mercy, ye abject wretches, the outcasts of the nations of the earth, are treated here with tenderness and humanity. And I wish I could not say, with too great indulgence also, for you have grown wanton with excess liberty, and your idleness has proved your ruin, having given you the opportunities of forming this villainous and detestable conspiracy. A scheme compounded of the blackest and foulest vices, treachery, blood-thirstiness, and ingratitude. Be not deceived, God Almighty only can and will proportion punishments to men's offences."

The punishment of man assessed: Cuffee and Quack were

to be taken the next day to the stake and burnt alive for their crimes against white people.

The crowd gathered for the execution was massive, over-whelming, boisterous. They had come to see blood, Negro blood, to see meat broiled on the bone. To witness the source of their suspicion and terror now burning itself in hateful fires. Despite the impending doom of the condemned, Cuffee and Quack's captors never ceased in trying to get the two men to confess to their crimes.

"Your eternal souls are in the balance," the white men in charge told them. "There is still a chance to save yourselves from such a horrific demise—or at least this day from it."

At about three o'clock, the two convicted were brought to the stake. The split wood was set out and piled high, ready to claim their bodies once they were tied above it. The people, many of whom had arrived hours before, were impatient, screaming at the top of their lungs for the show to begin, call-ing openly to the doomed men for retribution. Mr. Moore and Mr. John Roosevelt, a butcher at the Fly Market, led Cuf-fee and Quack to their fate, taking notice that both seemed as petrified about the upcoming event as the crowd seemed hungry for it. Sensing the two captives' willingness to talk, yet the reluctance of each to be the first to begin, their captors had the bright idea to break the two Africans up, and question them individually.

It worked.

At the brink of being burned alive, and thinking that his fellow had already saved his own skin by declaiming freely, each man cracked, spewing desperate, last-second confessions. Their white captors struggled to hear their words over the bloodthirsty roar of the crowd. Dictating their admissions for prosperity as the mob screamed and waved for murder just beyond.

"John Hughson started everything," Quack cried, hoping against hope that this information would save him. " 'Twas Hughson that brought Caesar and Prince and Cuffee for the scheming of it, along and twenty others."

Those twenty other poor souls, the desperate Quack proceeded to doom one by one, providing their names to Butcher Roosevelt.

"Hughson wanted what the Negroes could bring to his house from the fires, bragging that he would bring in more enslaved by the boatload from the country to assist their plan."

Quack was asked, "What view did Hughson have in acting in this manner?"

"To make himself rich," came the African's desperate response. Quack said there were around fifty involved in the conspiracy, although he didn't have names for them all. For Sandy and Fortune, though, he had special admonishment.

"They were as involved as any, and that Sandy can name the Spanish Negroes who as a group had been involved."

As so many had accused him, Quack even admitted to the firing of the fort.

"At eight P.M. that night, with a lighted stick taken out of the servants' hall I did do it," Quack offered, convinced that nothing but a complete acceptance of guilt would do. "I went up the back stairs to a top bedroom, sticking it outside in a gutter."

Fearing for his own safety in this suspicious time, the sentry guard, John McDonald, emerged from the crowd and stormed the stage during the confession to demand his own name be cleared before these judges focused their mad gaze on him.

"Tell them! Tell them my own confession was honest," McDonald demanded of the condemned man.

"It was true, he told the truth," the broken Quack managed through his tears. "I also tried to light the fort up the night before the fire, on Saint Patrick's Day while the troops drank, but the firebrand I placed in the garret had failed to catch. But my wife, she is innocent. Please, sirs, she should be pardoned."

Cuffee's confession mirrored Quack's in regard to the guilt of Hughson, the size of the conspiracy, and the hypocritical nature of Fortune and Sandy, the latter of whom had ties to the Spanish Negroes. Cuffee added more to the post as well, including his own confession as to Philipse's storehouse.

"I ran from the boat I was working on when Adolph Philipse went to the coffeehouse, then sprint back to the storehouse with a lit ember held in my pocket inside an oyster shell. Then I placed it by the ropes and boards in the storehouse and then came running home again," he told them.

That was all good, but that was just the petty act of one slave toward his master, what of the great conspiracy?

"Many who had been planning are worried they will now be discovered because last winter a constable [Constable North, it was later identified] broke up our meeting at Hughson's and had seen *all* of us," Cuffee added.

In the end, as historical document, in the written accounts by their separate interrogators, Quack and Cuffee's confessions are so similar that it's clear that Butcher Roosevelt and Mr. Moore were checking each other's progress, putting them together to avoid contradiction.

Amid the yells and chaos, the stories given were considered satisfactory. As he had promised the terrified slaves, Mr. Moore asked the sheriff to delay the execution until the governor could be notified that the guilty parties were now turning into witnesses for the King. It seemed at last that Cuffee and Quack would be saved, having finally found a sliver of mercy in the white man's judicial system.

While the crowd, annoyed by the delay, continued to roar, Mr. Moore met with His Honor to present this new situation. Unfortunately, before the two slaves could be removed from harm's way, the sheriff came to the decision that it didn't matter what the judge said or promised, informing Moore of his decision on his return.

"We can't do that," Moore argued. "We promised these boys we'd spare them if they talked."

"Do you see this crowd?" was the sheriff's argument. "Do *you* want to go out there and tell them their fun's been canceled?"

The mob wanted blood. Looking out at the ragtag assemblage, the brave officers of the court decided it would be in their best interest to give it to them.

So despite their confessions, it was back to the stake for Cuffee and Quack. Despite all their oath-breaking, backstabbing, and name-naming, the condemned had only bought themselves a few minutes more in their wretched existence.

The execution finally commenced, to the exuberant delight of the assembly who had come, after all, to rejoice in the spectacle, and the guilty relief of the cowards behind it. The wood was set ablaze, and the Africans' skin started roasting, as the men struggled on the stake to avoid the white cloud that enveloped and would suffocate them as their spirits left their scorched flesh.

Cuffee and Quack burned, painfully and publicly, betrayed and betrayers. They died, steamed by their own fluids, as they experienced a bit of that white benevolence that the court judge had just admonished them for spurning.

THIS IS THAT HUGHSON!

I F CAPTAIN LUSH dost not send us to our own country, we will ruin all the city. The first house we will burn will be his, spite him."

Sandy claimed he heard six of the Spanish Negroes saying as much as he was passing innocently by Captain Lush's home two weeks before the fort fire. It was in this way, he said, that he first discovered the plot.

"They did not see me, as I hid in a neighbor's doorway and listened," Sandy told the judges. His was an improbable story: Sandy contended that he had only just happened to be there, that the conspirators failed to check around them before having such a sensitive conversation, and even that these Spanish slaves would conspire in English.

After Saturday's excitement, Cuffee and Quack's charcoaled remains had cooled to the touch. The scent of meat that had been men lingered in the air causing still more tongues to loosen in the wake of its aroma. Monday began with a whole new round of storytelling, and Sandy was scrambling to pay for his life with any scrap of information in which the court might find interest. Now he told a grand tale of a conspiratorial meeting held by Jack at the home of his enslaver, Gerardus Comfort. This time Sandy just happened to be passing by when Jack called to him. To hear Sandy tell it, he was the quintessential innocent, an utterly passive fellow, fallen into the wrong crowd. In fact, he said he would not even drink with the others when offered.

In Sandy's version, six Spanish Negroes were present, along with a dozen other enslaved blacks, improbably packed into the small colonial room. Some of the names he recounted were of those already in jail or killed for their part, but there were some new names thrown in for good measure as well.

As the other conspirators looked on, Jack unfolded a dust cloth, revealing about a dozen knives. One by one, Sandy recalled, Jack started passing the knives around the room. The blades were old, poorly cared for, and covered in the brown decay of rust, looking like they'd been stored in a damp well for decades.

"What are these supposed to be? You couldn't cut porridge with this bunch," one of the enslaved complained.

Jack purportedly ignored the criticism, and kept delivering his favors across the room. "My knife is so sharp," he countered, "that if it came across a white man's head, it would cut it off."

Sandy said when Jack tried to hand him a blade, he told him, "If you want to fight, go to the Spaniards and not fight with your masters."

"Help me, we shall burn down the houses and take the city," Sandy swore Jack insisted of him.

Sandy told the court his response was to start *crying*.

"Damn you, do you cry?" Sandy said Jack responded. "I'll cut off your head in a hurry."

"He'd deserve it," Sandy recalled Sarah joined in, as the rest surrounded him,

"The plan will work and we will be victors," Jack insisted, "though I worry we won't have enough men till next year. So we shall do this as such: Each will burn down his own master's house before moving on to burn the rest," he instructed.

"We shall kill all the white men, and have their wives to ourselves," the others rejoiced.

"We must swear then, that if any of you discover, the first thunder that comes will strike you dead if you do not stand to your words," Sandy insisted Jack warned before the conspirators broke up and went their separate ways that evening.

Burk's Sarah, the only woman Sandy had named in the conspiracy, and the one of whom he had spoken so disparagingly, was pulled before the court for examination. Sarah's reaction to the line of questioning was to start uttering fierce denials.

According to Horsmanden, Sarah "threw herself into the most violent agitations; foamed at the mouth" as the judges tried to place her within the web of the plot. "A creature of outrageous spirit," Horsmanden pronounced her.

It wasn't until Sandy's denouncement of her was read back to the court that Sarah, realizing her predicament, joined in the spirit of things, and started naming slaves for the court to persecute next.

Fully aware what her fate would be if she did not cooperate, Sarah went from complete stalwart denial to naming more than thirty names over the course of the next few minutes. She named so many individuals that, when the group was read back to her, even she realized it wasn't even realistic, so promptly removed a dozen from the list.

By the end of the day on June 1, 1741, fifty-six enslaved Africans had been incarcerated. Fifty-six people since the original arrests for that minor burglary now almost faded into the irrelevance. Each new person seized was made to understand that if they did not come up with a confession, they would pay the same price as the first four. Each new name named added to the court's list, meant the trial's scope was destined to keep growing.

And so it did.

Around the same time that June afternoon, the under-sheriff came down the hall with a message to the court recorder—none other than Daniel Horsmanden himself—that Hughson wanted to speak to one of the judges, he was finally ready to do some talking. Not sharing the information, Horsmanden chose to go to Hughson's jail cell himself a few hours later.

"What do you want with the judges?" Horsmanden demanded of him. He would not have these important gentlemen bothered, nor taken off track by mere unimportance.

"Is there a Bible? I desire to be sworn," Hughson said to him.

"No oath will be administered to you. If you have anything to say, you have free liberty to speak. You've lived a wicked life, John Hughson, doing wicked practices: debauching and corrupting of Negroes, and encouraging them to steal and pilfer from their masters and others. For shame, you showed your children so wicked an example, training them up in the highway to hell."

All this morality from a man who in later years would go on to marry a wealthy woman in her seventies just to pay off his personal debts.

"God will give you no mercy for this matter," Horsmanden concluded his lecture, telling the deflated Hughson the court would be offering no mercy either.

It was a screed that would ensure that no confession from John Hughson would follow, and none did. After Horsmanden's long speech had ended, Hughson was left to stare blankly at him through unseeing eyes.

Smiling softly, he now declared, "I know nothing of this conspiracy. With God as my witness."

★ ★ ★

John Hughson would have his voice heard soon enough, however, along with his wife, Sarah, and their daughter of the same name, as well as the tavern's boarder, Peggy Kerry. Just a few days later, on Thursday, the fourth of June, the group was escorted to court to face the charges against them.

"Not guilty," came back their plea.

"You, the prisoners at the bar," the court clerk addressed them, "we must inform you that the law allows you the liberty of challenging peremptorily twenty of the jurors, if you have any dislike to them, and you need not give your reasons for doing so."

The prisoners decided amongst themselves that it would be John Hughson to do the challenging. Hughson, the only male, playing the role of patriarch, quickly showed how effective he would be in the group's defense when he decided to kick off the jury the lone young merchant amid a coterie of older, settled choices.

Peggy Kerry immediately objected to his action. "You've challenged one of the best of them all!" she fumed in disgust, causing laughter among the spectators close by enough to hear her.

The indictments were now set forth. The three adults stood accused of consorting with Negroes, gathering them in a conspiracy to burn the city down and kill its inhabitants. It was time for the case to begin in full. Rumors and accusations had flown freely in regard to John Hughson and his cohorts for months, but now the day of reckoning had finally arrived.

The prosecutor knew the crowd's anticipation and precon-
ceptions, knew how to harness them.

"Gentlemen," the prosecutor exhorted, "such a monster
will this Hughson appear before you, that for the sake of the
plunder he expected by setting in flames the King's house, and
this whole city, and by effusion of the blood of his neighbors,
he murderous and remorseless he! [*sic*] counseled and encourage the committing of all these most astonishing deeds of
darkness, cruelty, and inhumanity—Infamous Hughson!"

The tiny hairs on the back of the neck of his listeners rose
to attention at the enormity of it all.

"Gentlemen, this is that Hughson! Whose name and most
detestable conspiracies will no doubt be had in everlasting re-
membrance, to his eternal reproach; and stand recorded to latest posterity. This is the man! This that grand incendiary!
That arch rebel against God, his king, and his country! The
Devil incarnate, and chief agent of the old Abaddon of the
internal pit, and Geryon of darkness."

Because testimony from slaves against whites was inadmissi-
ble in court, the near-death confessions of Cuffee and Quack
were technically worthless. Technicalities, however, could be
worked in the prosecution's favor when court and prosecutor
were one and the same. Most of the damning testimony naming Hughson as the lead conspirator had come from slaves
Cuffee and Quack, but it had been told to white men. Mr.
Moore and Butcher Roosevelt were now called to relay the
secondhand evidence of Cuffee and Quack as if it was their

own: that Hughson was the first contriver and promoter. That Mary Burton spoke the truth and could speak more.

Following directly upon these testimonies, constables Joseph North and Peter Lynch were called to the stand to speak about the night in which they interrupted a group at Hughson's Tavern, a night that Cuffee had mentioned in his dying words. The constables had seen all who were involved in the plot and could discover the entire group. The constables attested they had found Peggy Kerry serving blacks and drove off the meeting of Negroes with the lashes of their canes.

"There was a cabal of Negroes at Hughson's last Whitsuntide," the two constables related. "Ten, twelve, or fourteen of them." *Fourteen slaves.* Fourteen at the most were at Hughson's when they broke up the party. Yet Cuffee had said "all those involved" were there at the scene, and Cuffee's own forced confession had around *fifty* involved altogether—which built on the existing understanding that there had been twenty to thirty, as put forth by Mary Burton.

The Hughsons and Peggy Kerry listened to the testimony without any notable emotion or interference. It wasn't until Mary Burton took to the stand that the accused clan started to lose whatever minor sense of hope to which they might still have been clinging. Mary Burton told her usual tales, given in a now-perfected performance of sympathy. It was damning testimony, but the Hughsons didn't hear it: immediately after Mary Burton started giving her evidence, John and his wife started crying.

Not just crying, wailing. Wailing loudly and without shame.

Demonstratively, for all to see, they hugged and kissed their daughter Sarah in utmost and heart-rending despair.

"I took great care in raising my daughter, as well as the rest of my children," John suddenly blurted to the court. "Teaching them to read the Bible, and breeding them up in the fear of the Lord."

Wife Sarah, for her part, at this moment brought her nursing infant from the crowd to her breast to invoke added empathy. The baby was ordered by the court to be taken away.

After such disturbance, Mary was ordered to resume her testimony and went on. She named additional names, telling of the many oaths to secrecy she had overheard.

"Hughson swore the Negroes into the plot," she said. "And the Hughsons swore themselves and Peggy. One of the Hughsons' daughters carried a Bible upstairs—"

"Now you are found out in a great lie!" Mrs. Hughson shouted at her through her tears. "For we never had a Bible in the world!"

The room got a good laugh out of that statement, the comment coming as it did minutes after her husband's biblical assertions.

Regardless of the momentary interruption, and lightness in the crowd, Mary Burton's testimony demanded their reattention.

"John Hughson handed out seven or eight guns and swords, gunpowder and shot included. The slaves were to cut their masters' and mistresses throats," Mary claimed. "Hughson was to be king and Caesar governor," Mary repeated to the jury.

"They had sworn to kill me, to burn and destroy me if I made their scheme public, but that hasn't stopped me. They bribed me with silks and gold rings, but still they did not prevail."

Perhaps as damning as the words being spoken inside the courthouse at the moment was the action taking place outside. Some time after the trial began that day, yet another of Philipse's outbuildings was mysteriously set afire, this time a horse stable.

Again, the quick questions, and harder conclusions. Was it meant as distraction so that the nefarious gang might effect an escape? Were the hot brands that lit the blaze left by precarious accident, or was this act, too, part of the greater plan?

Whether calculated or not, the blaze did nothing to stop the trial's proceedings. Mary Burton was followed to the stand by Arthur Price, having warmed up on Negroes and now ready to give testifying against whites a try. Again came hearsay, second-party, slave testimony of questionable legality, yet again ignored by Hughson's band, who failed to challenge with questions of their own to in any way refute the evidence being given against them.

The witnesses called by the accused prisoners (for they, of course, were handling their own defense, able to afford no lawyer, nor, probably, capable to find one willing, even if they had the money) were completely ineffectual. One, the poor, white wife of a sailor, made the implausible claim that she had never seen any Negroes besides Cuffee at Hughson's at all during her two-month stay there. Another man, again white, said he saw Hughson serve alcohol to blacks, "but thought him a civil man." A final witness said he saw no harm in John Hughson but he "knew nothing of the character of Hughson's house."

Perhaps the most sympathetic testimony of the trial came from a witness for the King, a former neighbor who said he often chastised Hughson for his late-night revelries. The neighbor complained, after one such night of debauchery, he spoke once more to Hughson about the offending behavior.

"It's my wife, isn't it?" the witness reported Hughson told him. "She dragged me away from my quiet country life of farming and shoemaking for the chance at more money in the city, but my gains have been so small, and my family so large, that they soon run away with what we have. My wife, she's the chief cause of having the Negroes in the house."

"The witnesses declare," Horsmanden clarified for all still unable to discern, "the principal contriver of those mischiefs to be that wicked man, John Hughson, whose crimes have made him blacker than a Negro: the scandal of his complexion, and the disgrace of human nature! Whose name will descend with infamy to posterity!"

At that point, the judge informed the jury they had all the pertinent information needed, and that now they needed to make their decision.

"But on the other hand," the judge continued, "as the evidence against them seems to be so ample, so full, so clear and satisfactory, if you have no particular reason in your own breasts, in your own consciences, to discredit them, if that, I say, is not the case, if you have no reason to discredit them, then I make no doubt but you will discharge a good conscience, and find them guilty."

And so the jury did, wasting very little time at it.

John Hughson and his wife, Sarah, along with Peggy Kerry, were convicted of three guilty indictments, daughter Sarah of two. The self-righteous, racial indignation of the good white people of the city of New York was on full display as the sentence was handed down.

As it turned out, it was John Hughson's failure as a traitor to whiteness that was as much his crime as the more fanciful charges alleged against him.

"Yours are indeed as singular, and unheard of before, they are such as one would scarce believe any man capable of committing, especially any one who had heard of a God and a future state; for people who have been brought up and always lived in a Christian country, and also called themselves Christians, to be guilty not only of making Negro slaves their equals, but even their superiors, by waiting upon, keeping with, and entertaining them with meat, drink, and lodging, and what is much more amazing, to plot, conspire, consult, abet, and encourage these black seed of Cain to burn this city, and to kill and destroy us all. Good God!"

The three whites were sentenced to be hanged by the neck until "severely dead" on June 12, 1741. After death, the infamous John Hughson was still to receive special treatment. His corpse was to be removed from its noose and rehung in chains next to the body of his nefarious slave comrade.

Caesar's corpse silently awaited the company.

Four days later, on the day of his scheduled execution, Hughson declared from his jail cell, "I deserve death for the stealing of Hogg's property, but as to the rest! As for the rest I am innocent!"

It was good that John Hughson could agree, at least in part, to his sentence, but regardless, he was about to die. That much was obvious, foregone, and highly anticipated.

"Yet listen to my prophecy—a great sign from God will occur to prove me so," he insisted.

"Just come out of your cell, John Hughson," the guard ordered. "You will have all the audience you desire on this day."

John Hughson emerged from his cell with his head held high. Not simply to show his enduring pride, but also to show off his latest affectation: two shilling-size red marks on his face, one adorning each cheek. It was a painful bit of performance art, shoving his dirty and ragged fingernails into the tender flesh of his rum-softened face, but it was worth the effort. As the crowd turned out to watch the condemned be pulled down the road in open carriage, the sight of John's self-inflicted stigmata sent the spectators atitter with the spectacle. A great preview of things to come.

Finally given an opportunity to truly play to the crowd, Hughson made sure that the citizens of this New York would have a good look at him in his majesty, standing in his cart the whole way to his hanging. He had become a symbol, and knowing that performed as one literally.

"Sit your bloody arse down, are things not as bad as they can be?" his wife beseeched him, but he remained undaunted. One hand straight up in the air as high as he could manage, his forefinger pointing as a beacon, John Hughson became a vision to be remembered, as surely as he intended.

"Will you look at that, he marks his destination in the heavens above, making his peace with the God he knows," came a whisper through the crowd.

"Don't be a fool—he's signaling for his rescuers, for the revolution to begin!" Darting eyes swept the street searching for the first glimpse of the apocalyptic mob of armed Africans.

But none appeared. The wheels on the horse-drawn cart bounced forward on the uneven cobblestone road without halting. John Hughson kept his finger in the air, but no dark hordes would come to his rescue. The wheels on that cart did not stop until they reached the gallows.

His wife, Sarah, was resigned, immobile, "a lifeless trunk," as the coarse hemp rope was placed around her neck and then thrown over a stout tree limb. Despite her cooperation and confession, Peggy Kerry found herself right beside her. The crowd, for its part, roared. "We die as innocents," Peggy declared. "We know nothing of this conspiracy which has been imagined. It not be more true for our deaths."

And then the rope went taut, and the three had nothing more to say in the matter.

Legs kicked. Bodies spun. Pendular mortality giving its parting dance, and the crowd cheering at the sight of it. Quieting only to witness the next victims, slaves Albany, Curaçao Dick, and Francis, fitted for their own nooses.

In death all motion stilled. John Hughson's lifeless body was cut down. As prescribed, only to be restrung in chains for permanent display alongside Caesar's. Mates in life, death, and history.

"I'VE BEEN A SLAVE
LONG ENOUGH"

THE CITY OF NEW YORK had gotten so good at killing Negroes, they were doing them five at a time. Peck's Caesar, Gomez's Cuffee, Comfort's Cook, Comfort's Jack, Ellison's Jamaica were brought to trial together. Men without whole names, their very identities enslaved by their masters'. They were marched in together and this was how they were convicted as well, largely on the death scene confessions of Cuffee and Quack as told via Mr. Moore and Mr. John Roosevelt once more. Black confessions, born under duress, now filtered through the voices of white men for the appearance of legality. The court had lost its façade as balancer of guilt and innocence.

Sandy appeared again on the witness stand and told the judges, "Peck's Caesar bragged to me, 'I'll kill the white men and drink their blood to their good health.'"

By now Sandy had grown accustomed to testifying in front of the court, liking quite well the attention and personal safety it offered him. In fact, Sandy liked talking so much that even after his final appearance was over, and he was being shipped out of town and far away, he was still yapping, his tale growing so large and extravagant with each retelling, that some of his shipmates believed that the trials had only touched the tip of the bother.

Five Africans brought in front of the New York court of inquisition, five guilty verdicts waiting to be pronounced. Only Jamaica proved to have any mitigating circumstances.

"Jamaica is not concerned that I know of, but he was frequently at Hughson's with his fiddle," Quack had declared in his final, desperate confession. The magistrates chose to ignore Quack's dying words, however. Thanks to Mary Burton.

"Oh yes, I know that one," she declared. "He said he'd dance or play over the whites while they were roasting in flames. 'I've been a slave long enough,' was what he said."

Still, in the end Jamaica was the fortunate one. While his fellow enslaved were quickly sentenced to be chained and burned at the stake, Jamaica was spared the torture. Instead, he was sentenced to a relatively comfortable hanging. A considerable break, since by giving up others, Jamaica was able to convert his sentence into expulsion to the West Indies.

The more slaves brought in, the more names named. The more names named, the more slaves brought in. The more slaves brought in, the more the story grew. And grew. And grew.

In just a few months, half of the city's male slaves over the age of sixteen had been implicated in the plot.

Antonio de St. Bendito, Antonio de la Cruz, Pablo Ventura Angel, Juan de la Sylva, Augustine Gutierez, Spanish blacks all, pled not guilty before the court, as if their pleas mattered. Insisting that their *real* surnames be used and not the names of their kidnappers, the group was clearly not attempting to endear themselves to the jury. For these men, their time in front of the court was opportunity to finally discuss their unlawful slavery.

Cuffee and Quack had said that Sandy could tell the court about the Spanish Negroes, and Sandy did not disappoint. Neither did Comfort's Jack or Mr. Moore, who was called to the stand to repeat Cuffee's and Quack's confessions.

"Damn that son of a bitch. If he does not carry us to our own country, we will ruin the city and play the devil with him," Antonio de St. Bendito, pointing to Captain Lush's house, was said to have muttered to the other Spanish enslaved.

"We'll burn Captain Lush's house with him tied to a beam inside it, roast him like a piece of beef," de St. Bendito allegedly continued to strategize. "Let us stay in New York for a month and a half to wait for the Spanish to arrive. If they did not come, we'll begin taking control of the island by ourselves."

Sandy said he heard his contribution just passing by the Spanish Negroes as they were speaking to each other. It's an interesting excuse. Question: why would these men be speaking to one another about such a sensitive topic in *English*, loud enough for a random passerby like Sandy to hear them? Either Sandy was lying about hearing anything, or lying about his own involvement. The court didn't care which one. The court didn't care about anything but confirming their own nightmare. That there was a sleeper cell ready to take the city down in blood and fire.

The issue of whether the accused Spanish blacks were even legal slaves at all was brushed aside with the testimony of a sailor who swore that he had traveled with Antonio de St. Bendito's brother. The sailor claimed that he knew a man who had bought Antonio's brother in Havana, relaying assurances that the African's family was from Cartagena, and all were slaves. This third-party account from a man of foreign birth and residency, completely unknown, to the court was all they required to damn all of the "Spanish Negroes."

Realizing he was about to be relieved of his hefty investment, Antonio de St. Bendito's enslaver, merchant Peter De Lancey, jumped in to try and protect his investment.

"It may interest the court that my Antonio was away from the city, north at my farm in the country, during much of the time in question," the merchant began. "It should also be known that Antonio had also suffered from frostbitten feet and was completely lame at the time, not returning to the city until after the fort was burnt."

In light of this revelation, the court considered excluding Antonio de St. Bendito from the sentencing. But then the master of Antonio de la Cruz stepped forward with an almost identical alibi, declaring that his slave had been completely homebound with frostbitten toes from November to the middle of March.

Then a witness for Pablo Ventura Angel forswore that *he* had been sick until March. By the time a witness for Augustine Gutierez declared that he had suffered in February from ague, the health excuses were so worn as to render them all ineffectual.

It took a half hour to convict the lot of them.

The question of whether the men were even slaves in the first place was finally dealt with by selling them all to slave traders headed for the West Indies. It was the opinion of the court of New York that these Spanish blacks could go argue for their freedom elsewhere.

In the end, approximately one hundred and sixty of New York island's Africans would be thrown into jail and questioned. Seventy-two would be banished from the life they had known in the colony altogether, forced to start over again in the tropical islands to the south or on the Portuguese coastal island of Madeira. Eighteen would feel the coarse rope of the noose tighten around their necks. Thirteen would be publicly roasted alive for the pleasure of the crowd. Fire having begat fire, their only fortune was to die poetically.

"HE SEEMED VERY LOATH
TO DO IT"

NEGROES WERE STUPID CREATURES, servile, childish, incapable of higher thought—common knowledge not worthy of debate in the enlightened year of 1741. That said, like children they were prone to their tantrums, their outbursts, their petty acts of rebellion; any slaveholder could tell you that. This was the knowledge that informed the direction of the court in these trying times, but this was also the contradiction. How could a group of incompetents such as composed this blackened race manage to convene a conspiracy of such stunning size and complexity? It was inconceivable. Everyone knew it was scientifically impossible that hundreds of the infantile, bestial Negroes could have organized themselves to such purposes. One only need read David Hume's recently published essays to find expert proof of that. God had placed the Negro, like the ox or the hen, on earth to serve white man's needs. The truth was, therefore, inescapable. There must be a conniving white man behind all the chaos. Someone whose fair skin hid a dark heart beneath.

Someone so powerful as to make the Africans turn against their own divinely ordained nature.

John Hughson, certainly, could not be that person. John Hughson was a buffoon, a bumpkin, a low-class fool barely able to imitate humanity during his own trial. There was no way he could have been the maestro. What this case needed, what this ambitious court needed, was to capture the mesmeric genius who all the other testimony hinted at. This true ringleader must be found, this shadow conspirator whose tentacles took such great hold that even doomed slaves had kept his name snugly under their dying tongues.

So, Horsmanden and the assembled judges of the colony of New York were forced to ask themselves who would that perfect villain be? Of what must the man be composed? That he would be male was beyond question. That he was a stranger to the city—for how could one of their own possibly be guilty of such a heinous atrocity—was most probable, someone new to the area who had brought the trouble with him. That he would be a true God-fearing person was highly questionable. No, he would surely be a heathen, or even worse, a papal spy. An emissary sent to the New World by the pope himself to continue the Vatican's quest for global domination.

Into this situation walked John Ury.

John Ury, British-born schoolteacher, had recently arrived from Philadelphia. A modest but intellectual man of limited resources, of late he'd formed a business with Mr. Campbell, the schoolmaster, teaching their pupils classical linguistics. With few friends and a prudish, bookish manner that didn't endear him to the masses in this rough town, in the brief time he'd been in the city, John Ury had kept pretty much to himself. Most people who saw him would have taken little note. Now the court turned their attention to this slight man and observed: *A stranger!* And even more ominous to the judges, a stranger who taught and, therefore, spoke *Latin*. An almost definite indicator that the man was a Roman spy sent to overthrow the island in the name of the Catholic Church.

In light of such overwhelming evidence, John Ury was grabbed off the street and, after "not giving a satisfactory account of himself," thrown in jail.

Mary Burton was brought in the next day to seal the indictment for the prosecution. Burton had, since her first manipulated confession, proven herself continually helpful to the court. In fact, Mary Burton had been so extraordinarily helpful, that the initial group of some two dozen Africans she'd made reference to had now grown so far beyond her initial description that the sheer number of them would have made it physically impossible for all of them to fit into any single colonial home or even outbuilding at the same time—but why fret the details?

Despite the fact that she had once claimed that the only whites in Hughson's tavern were the proprietor himself and his wife, Romme, and Peggy Kerry, Mary Burton now expanded the list to include John Ury, per the court's most earnest beseechment. The judges were very thorough in the matter, bringing Burton through in the morning to view Ury in his cell to make sure she got a good look at the man. Despite this effort to educate the witness before the fact, Mary, in her later testimony, had trouble getting the name right.

"Yes, it was him," she pointed, declaring, "that man Mr. Jury that I had seen."

The prosecutors exchanged looks among themselves, understandably a bit uncomfortable for the moment.

"Miss Burton, are you sure about that, about the name of the accused?"

"Oh?" looking around as to astutely gauge the room, "No, no, I am mistaken. 'Twas another. It was, maybe Doyle. Yes, Doyle."

Mary faced the sudden rustling of the court, that look of disapproval she had previously avoided, and shifted again.

"No, not Doyle," she stammered. "That was not it, I remember now. But it was something. I recall clearly now. Some of his names had . . . one syllable."

In the end, Mary decided that the man suspected of being a Roman Catholic priest went by all three names, and that she'd seen him conspiring with Hughson since Christmas last. Not wanting to take all credit for the death sentence she had handed this man, Mary parted with a statement that the remaining Hughson detainee, daughter Sarah, had waited on him more than she, and could help the prosecution further.

As pathetic as this latest condemnation was, it was still possible that, after the immediate fervor subsided, John Ury might have been released. Even for these compromised proceedings, Mary Burton's testimony had been woefully inadequate, particularly when it was to decide the fate of a white Englishman.

John Ury's problems, however, extended beyond Mary Burton.

Two weeks later, Will, once enslaved by Mr. Ward, was in the process of being prepared to roast alive after his own guilty conviction when he came to that last resort, what had become that rather common and banal idea of the moment: confession. The unique innovation that Ward's Will brought back to the game of self-preservation was that having heard the rumors and talk scuttling through the cells, he added Europeans back into the realm of the suspect. Slaves were still legally forbidden from testifying against whites, but the executioner's pit was surely not a court of law, and anyway what be law in times of terror?

"Kane and another soldier, Edward Kelly, asked Quack to burn the fort so that they would be free of their obligation," Will desperately declared. "Even Kane's wife is guilty. She once pawned a stolen silver spoon. He did not care if the fort was burnt down."

Will talked and talked, and the sheriff, for his part, paused to listen. And Will was right, his confession bought him time. Time enough for the executioner to stoke a good fire beneath where he was held. Tied with his back to the stake, Will lifted his legs one at a time from the fire as long as he could, his confessional cries eventually being replaced by cries of agony. Will was talking, then he was screaming, then he was burning.

Raising his arms and eyes to the heavens above he cried for
mercy. But no mercy came.

William Kane was a forty-year-old soldier in the British Royal
Service. Born in Athlone, Ireland, he now found himself incarcerated and bound before the court of New York.

"'Tis true, I took part in the stolen spoon bit, but I've never
been at Hughson's establishment in my life," Kane insisted.

"Then you deny that you are a conspirator in the recent uprising, that you do not take orders directly from your Catholic
pope?"

"I owe allegiance only to the Church of England, sirs. I am
a Protestant born and lived, and have never had any associa-
tion with the Papists."

Kane was adamant, insistent, and by coming clean on his
surely provable guilt in regard to the stolen silver spoon incident, seemed to be setting a believable defense for himself
in regard to the most serious charges. It might have actually
worked, too, if Mary Burton had not been in the building,
poised to make yet one more accusatorial appearance.

In the middle of William Kane's impassioned denial, a sudden outburst interrupted the courtroom, putting a stop to the
proceedings. The under-sheriff addressed the judges. "Mary
Burton, gentlemen, is outside the courtroom declaring that
she had often seen William Kane at the Hughsons', too."

The judges ordered Mary brought back into the courtroom, where she immediately began repeating her accusations.

"He'd been consorting with them," Mary insisted when called to the stand. "With the blacks, talking of conspiracy!" It was another remarkably coincidental memory recall on behalf of young Mary, but for once it did not go unnoticed.

In what Horsmanden would later describe as "*an awful and solemn manner*," the chief justice, a recent addition to the proceedings after having been away on a special commission in Providence, interrupted Burton.

"Must I inform you, young girl, as to the nature of an oath, and to the consequences of taking a false one?" the senior official warned.

"Thank you, sir, but I know exactly what I'm doing," Mary continued self-righteously.

At first, William Kane continued to insist upon his innocence in regard to the conspiracy. There is hope in all of us that the truth is our greatest defense, and Kane clung to this until it was made perfectly clear to him that this room wanted something different. "You must not flatter yourself with the least hopes of mercy," the prosecutor warned him, lest he get any ideas from the chief justice. "Your only salvation will be through confession."

There was nothing William Kane could do, but what had been done before. To betray everyone, even himself.

"[His] countenance changed, and being near fainting," Horsmanden noted. Kane went flush, weak in the face of the reality of his situation. Visibly, he paused to compose himself.

His life depended on a confession, a confession composed and strong enough, with performance to match, in order to save his life.

"May I have some water?" Kane requested, buying time, waiting for inspiration to strike.

Water swallowed, thoughts settled upon and composed, Kane declared, "I am ready to tell the truth now."

"Though at the same time he seemed very loath to do it," Horsmanden noted of the several hours of confession that followed.

William Kane did not disappoint, implicating several other whites as he wove these innocents into the newly tooled, general mythology of Hughson's sinister plan. Led by prosecutors, Kane would cooperatively corroborate this involvement of the recently arrested suspected papal spy John Ury to the mix, answering the court's leading questions, taking them exactly where they wanted to go.

It was John Jury! Yes, it was John Jury! John Jury had been training these whites in the dark arts of the Catholic Church.

John Ury was found guilty, and William Kane provided the damning testimony against him, even though he never could quite get his name right.

"SUCH A PARTICULAR
PERSON FORGOTTEN?"

B ECAUSE JOHN URY WAS WHITE, it would take
more than a few bits of questionable accusation from the
lips of William Kane and Mary Burton to bring him down. An
entire canvas had to be created to give the schoolteacher appro-
priately ominous credence. It would mean not only incriminating just him, but also incriminating those around him. John
Corry the dancing master? He was there, Kane verbally complied; he saw him at Hughson's all the time. Holt, another
dancing master, did he not do the same? Yes, he did, Kane again
agreed, despite the fact that the man, in his own deposition, denied *even knowing* John Ury. Edward Murphy? David Johnson?
There were lots of whites mentioned by Kane. By design, it
seemed, the larger the picture, the more difficult to deny

For John Ury's part, he tried just that, giving a sworn, written statement to be entered into the court's record:

John Ury, school-master, denies being any wise concerned in
the conspiracy for burning the town and killing the inhabitants,

says, that he never was any wise acquainted with John Hughson or his wife, or Margaret Kerry, nor did he ever see them in his life, to his knowledge.

Signed,
John Ury

Ury presented his case for innocence hopeful that his word carried enough weight to squash all doubts. Whether it did in fact do so became moot because only moments after Ury's proclamation William Kane took the stand to testify to the opposite.

"Jury was at John Hughson's with the dancing masters."

"Of this you are quite certain?" the chief judge prodded.

"Well, I must say, I never actually saw Jury with any of the slaves, but it was said to be so."

William Kane made a point to say that he had *never actually seen* John Ury with any of the slaves, as opposed to all those other whites he'd placed with the Africans. It was a minor nuance to a court that had little time for subtleties, but it was a fairly major gap for one whose life was still hanging in abeyance.

If John Ury—who had the distinct benefit over all of the others who had previously been prosecuted by this court thus far, given that he was both white and educated—had had only Mary Burton's and William Kane's accusations to contend with, he might have actually had the advantage in the proceedings. Unfortunately for Ury, however, the court had induced another white voice to join the chorus to his damning.

Considering their success in the past in procuring testimonies from deponents whose very life depended on complying with the court's wishes, there could be no better source than young and vulnerable Sarah Hughson. The girl had already seen the court put to death both her mother and father, but young Sarah remained alive on a stay of execution. Who had a better understanding of the comings and goings of John Hughson's pub but his own daughter? What other white person left still breathing would be as eager to save herself?

Despite all this, all she had to lose, Sarah remained defiant of the court. Repeated requests were sent to her to join in the condemnations of John Ury, and repeated refusals were returned. Sarah, lacking in years and racked by fear, still managed to hold out, rejecting any offer to damn more people to a similar fate. However, the weight of Sarah's own mortality came to a head on the date of the day of her impending execution. So finally, the last Hughson left in custody broke. The court now had what it wanted, a new funnel for its imagination.

"I had often seen Ury, the priest, at my father's house," Sarah told the judges. "He used to come there in the evenings and at night, and I have seen him in company with the Negroes." The testimony came strained, painfully, but once it started flowing it came creatively as well, the girl actively imagining what his Papist evil could be. To Sarah's mind, it must be dark. It must be arcane. It must be satanic, like the darkest whispered rituals.

"I have seen him several times make a round thing with chalk on the floor, and make all the Negroes then present stand round it," Sarah described. "He used to stand in the middle of the ring, with a cross in his hand, and there swore all the Negroes to be concerned in the plot, and that they should not discover him, nor any thing else of the plot, though they should die for it."

It was as everyone thought: Ury had been baptizing the Negroes and forgiving their every sin as well, just as Popish priests were known to. Without sin or fear of damnation, the beast that was the Negro was free to do anything. One could only shudder with the propensity of such thoughts.

The most detailed account of John Ury's life would come from Joseph Web, a carpenter and house joiner, who had hired Ury to tutor his children after overhearing him reading Latin (and noticing Ury looked a bit down on his luck). The picture Web constructed of the man was more mundane than menacing.

According to Web, John Ury had told him that he was an outcast from the Church of England who'd been run out of London after the publication of an unpopular pamphlet. That he'd come to New York looking for work after a brief stay in London. Ury could be heard to read prayers at night in the Church of England style. The only ambiguous marks Web made on John Ury's person were his testimony to the effect that Ury sometimes had a "dark, obscure, and mysterious manner," and that he'd once tried to buy some confectionary that wasn't shaped like animals, possibly looking for wafers for a sacrament.

"I was once ordained by a bishop of the Church of England,

and liked to preach, particular against drunkenness and debauchery of life," Web alleged Ury bragged.

In addition, Web said John Ury was also insistent that all who attended his little Bible studies be true to their own denomination, whether Presbyterian or Lutheran or Church of England. As for John Ury's relationship to Africans, Web relayed only one discussion.

"They have souls to be saved or lost as well as other people," the relatively progressive Joseph Web said he opined to the pious schoolmaster.

"They are not objects of salvation," John Ury replied.

"What would you do with them then, would you damn them all?"

"No," claimed John Ury. "Leave them to the Great Being that has made them, he knows best what to do with them. They are of a slavish nature, it is the nature of them to be slaves. Give them learning, do all the good you can, and put them above the condition of slaves, and in return they will cut your throats."

Despite evidence presented against John Ury's portrayal as the Great Black Leader, the court would hear none of it.

"Ury seemed to be well acquainted with the disposition of them," was Daniel Horsmanden's sole summation.

The trial of John Ury would take place on the twenty-ninth day of July, 1741. After the crier had cried, and the charge of leading the conspiracy been brought, it was again Mary Burton called to the stand.

"Mary, give the court and jury an account of what you know concerning the conspiracy to burn down the town and murder and destroy inhabitants, and what part you know the prisoner at the bar has acted in it," Mr. Chambers, the prosecutor, instructed her, careful to make sure his star witness handled this special occasion with care. "Tell the whole story from beginning, in your own method, but speak slow, not so hastily as you usually do, that the court and jury may the better understand you."

"Why, I have seen Ury very often at Hughson's about Christmas time and New Year, and then he stayed away about a fortnight or three weeks, and returned again about the time that Hogg's goods came to our house," Mary told the room, going on to place Ury at the tavern at all the important times. It was clear, according to Mary, Ury ministered to the whites while instructing the slaves to burn the fort, the Fly, and the city beyond. "I heard Ury tell them they need not fear doing it, for that he could forgive them their sins as well as God Almighty, and would forgive them."

Not to be outdone by Sarah Hughson, Mary brought in a new and creative ring to her story, one altogether menacing and supernatural. "After I was called upstairs by the schoolmaster, then dismissed, he was angry and shut the door to the room again." Mary squinted her eyes weirdly and peered around suspiciously before continuing. "I looked under it, and there was a black ring upon the floor, and things in it that seemed to look like rats."

"Rats?" the prosecutor repeated incredulously.

"I don't know what they were, but, yes, demon rats! But that is not all. One night, some time about New Year, I was listening at the door of the room upon the stairs, where there was Ury, Hughson, his wife and daughter Sarah, Vaarck's Caesar, Auboyneau's Prince, Philipse's Cuff, and other Negroes, and I looked up through the door and saw upon the table a black thing like a child."

The room hushed, gasps of air being sucked into silence. Mary leaned forward, her voice growing louder as she expanded upon this tale of horror.

"Ury had a book in his hand and was reading, but I did not understand the language. And having a spoon in my hand, I happened to let it drop upon the floor, and Ury came out of the room, running after me downstairs, and he fell into a tub of water."

It took some moments of digestion, before the judges were able to discern what Mary had purportedly seen. The demon rats, they decided, must have been *the Africans' toes*, obscured from her angle or perspective, she, after all, spying on them, peering under the door.

The judiciary made no attempt to seek an explanation for the second vision, this embryonic, black devil thing, "like a child," surely an incarnation of Beelzebub himself. More curious, neither did John Ury avail himself, he who now had chance to seek certitude, stepping to the fore in order to question Mary immediately after the prosecution had finished up with her.

While cross-examining Mary Burton, John Ury paced the

floor, ineffectually intent, although armed with opportunity, to expose this trial for the sham that it was, be done with the insanity, and clear his good name.

"You say you have seen me several times at Hughson's; what clothes did I usually wear?" Ury began.

"I cannot tell what clothes you wore particularly," Mary deflected.

"That is strange, and you know me so well."

"I have seen you in several clothes, but you chiefly wore a riding coat, and often a brown coat trimmed with black," Mary ventured.

"I have never worn any such coat!" John Ury turned to declare proudly to the court, a slight smile on his face that he'd caught her. "And let me ask you further, what was it the Negroes said in response to my supposed offer to wipe away their sins?"

"I'm sure I don't remember."

"You don't remember?" Ury declared. "That will be all," And that was it. There were no further questions.

John Ury might have been a very good Latin teacher. An excellent teacher, it is said, of Greek as well. But as a criminal defense attorney, he was truly pathetic—even when arguing verily for his own existence.

William Kane was called next, offering a far less sensational testimony, but one that still agreed on the points that mattered. John Ury had tried (and failed) to persuade Kane to become a Roman Catholic, and Kane had seen him baptize a child, Kane swore. Also, Kane said, he knew Ury to have connections with

Hughson, and said that there were slaves to be involved in the burning of the city. John Ury's rebuttal to this was to follow the same line of questioning he had pursued so ineffectually with Mary Burton.

"You say you have seen me very often, you saw me at Coffin's, you saw me several times at Hughson's; pray, what clothes did you see me in?" Ury asked Kane.

"I have seen you in black, I have seen you in a yellowish greatcoat, and sometimes in a straight-bodied coat, of much the same color."

To this Ury had no response. Did that mean he actually owned such clothes, the room wondered. Either way, did it matter? John Ury was trying to discredit the accusers by saying they had never seen him before and couldn't even remember his dress, but it wasn't physically impossible for people to change clothes (although, perhaps, financially impractical). If John Ury was a man who could control legions of rats, invoke monster babies, and cause the docile African to rise in armed rebellion, why wouldn't John Ury be able to scrounge up an extra coat?

"And you, what do you say as to the time that I was supposed to have frequented the public house of John Hughson's?"

"It was in the evening," William Kane responded. Again, it was a pointless line of questioning. When else was one likely to go to a tavern?

The schoolmaster did show a bit of acumen when Sarah Hughson was called to witness against him, showing he clearly was prepared, finally, in her regard.

"I except against her being sworn," Ury contested, "for she has been convicted, and received sentence of death for being concerned in this conspiracy, and, therefore, cannot be a witness."

Unfortunately for Ury, the court thought otherwise.

"But, Mr. Ury," the attorney general volleyed back, "she has received His Majesty's most gracious pardon, which she has pleaded in court this morning, and it has been allowed of, and, therefore, the law says, she is good evidence."

Yes, Sarah had been conveniently pardoned of her convicted crimes *that morning*, just in time to pass her death sentence on to another. And after that brief respite, Sarah did her testifying, basically repeating her deposition of days before.

Predictably, John Ury's response to Sarah Hughson's allegations were as ineffectual as his previous cross-examinations. All he managed was a rather tepid, quick exchange with Sarah concerning who he had supposedly baptized among the conspirators, and not even bothering to challenge her replies.

Yet, things were about to get even worse for John Ury. Hundreds of miles south, in the debtor's colony that was Georgia, General James Oglethorpe, the colony's original advocate and current leader, was in the middle of the War of Jenkins' Ear, as English Georgia fought it out with Spanish Florida. Under siege and headed for defeat, the beleaguered general sent a frantic note to the English colony of the north warning of impending doom.

Frederica, in Georgia, May 16, 1741.

Sir—A party of our Indians returned the eighth instant from war against the Spaniards; they had an engagement with a party of Spanish horse, just by Augustine, and brought one of them prisoner to me: he gives me an account of three Spanish sloops and a snow, privateers, who are sailed from Augustine to the northward, for the provision vessels, bound from the northward to the West-Indies, hoping thereby to supply themselves with flour, of which they are in want. Besides this account which he gave to me, he mentioned many particulars in his examination before our magistrates.

Some intelligence I had of a villainous design of a very extraordinary nature, and if true, very important, viz. that the Spaniards had employed emissaries to burn all the magazines and considerable towns in the English North-America, thereby to prevent the subsisting of the great expedition and fleet in the West-Indies: and that for this purpose, many priests were employed, who pretended to be physicians, dancing-masters, and other such kinds of occupations; and under that pretence to get admittance and confidence in families. As I could not give credit to these advices, since the thing was too horrid for any prince to order, I asked him concerning them; but he would not own he knew anything about them.

I am, sir, your very humble servant,

James Oglethorpe.

Superscribed,

To the honourable George Clarke-Esq.
Lieutenant Governor of New York

This letter proved a death knell for the unlucky John Ury. A proponent of debtors' rights and a staunch antislavery advocate who had so far kept Georgia slavery-free despite his colonists' wishes, James Oglethorpe was a respected leader in the American colonies. Unfortunately for John Ury, although Oglethorpe's paranoid warning was written in a completely different context and for a completely different purpose, in content it suited the New York court's fears and prejudices perfectly.

The letter was read in its entirety before the court, and John Ury's fate was further sealed in the process.

Refusing to submit or even address these outlandish accusations, Ury proceeded to bring forth a grouping of past employers and associates as character witnesses. People who had come to know him over the past few months, people who attested to his hours, and his devout religious nature as nonjuried member of the Church of England (even if they also confessed that they didn't quite understand what Ury was talking about). Through his former business associate, John Campbell, and his wife, the defendant was able to establish his only existing tie to Sarah Hughson: the fact that he had been with the couple weeks before when they came coincidentally to take up residence at the vacant house formerly let by John Hughson, only to be chased away by the bereaved daughter, Sarah Hughson, as she swore and cursed at these people for their perceived audacity to think they had the right to rent and move into the home once occupied by herself, her father, and her mother.

John Ury apparently had said to Sarah at the time, "How dare you talk so impertinently and saucily to an old woman, you impudent hussy! Go out of the house, or I will turn you out."

So he *had* already met Sarah Hughson, and in a manner those insults hurled might have given her more of a motive to testify falsely against him. Here was a powerful weapon John Ury could have used to challenge the damning testimony of young Sarah. A weapon which he again failed to use to defend himself, when the time was right to do so, instead wasting his time questioning Sarah about the specifics of the supposed baptism.

Still, John Ury managed a strong point in his closing argument.

"A priest, a joint contriver of firing a fort, a celebrator of masses, a dispenser of absolutions as it is said I am, so long passed by? Such a particular person forgotten? No, gentlemen, you must think and believe he would have been the next person after the discovery of the plot that would have been brought to the carpet."

The jury took the wisdom in this statement, as well as the excessively lengthy entreaty Ury offered them in regard to the stark differences between his form of Anglicanism and Roman Catholicism, and armed thusly went off to confer about the fate of this white stranger residing in their midst.

They came back fifteen minutes later with their verdict. John Ury was sentenced to hang on August 29.

"Fellow Christians," John Ury addressed them on the day of his execution, prepared to deliver his last sermon to the mortal world. "I am now going to suffer a death attended with ignominy and pain; but it is the cup that my heavenly father has put into my hand, and I drink it with pleasure, knowing that all that live godly in Christ Jesus must suffer persecution. And we must be made in some degree partakers of his sufferings before we can share in the glories of resurrection."

John Ury was given peace by his faith, and he clung to it as he went on to deny not just his crime, but to deny also the Catholic concept of absolution, and the disregard for the sanctity of community that the fires had displayed.

"Indeed, it may be shocking to some serious Christians that the holy God should suffer innocence to be slain by the hands of cruel and bloody persons. (I mean the witnesses who swore against me in trial.) Indeed, there may be reasons assigned for it, but as they say, that is one of the dark providences of the great God, in his wise, just and good government of this lower earth."

The statement was eloquent, composed, and pious. It would not, however, save John Ury from the noose—that found him brief moments after his speech concluded—but the words did manage to live longer than he did. The oration, as it was prepared by Ury in the weeks leading up to his trip to the gallows, made it back to some acquaintances in Philadelphia who printed it in its entirety, circulating the impassioned words as proof of the barbarity and backward nature of their neighbors to the north.

A white man had died. A white male life, the most sacred of God's creations, wasted. An educated, seemingly harmless free white man, sent to his maker.

Madness.

The fires had stopped. People were not so scared anymore. Rational thought was moving back into the territory, and people were reassessing the situation. The loss of white life. The loss of black property. So many slaves had been forfeited, taken into custody during the events, killed, or otherwise made useless to their owners. Bloodlust subsided, people started looking around, awakening from their haze.

Looking around now, assessing the damage, it was transparent to most—rich and poor alike—what had been lost.

That was clear. That was obvious.

But then, what exactly had been gained?

"PEOPLE WITH RUFFLES"

IN SPITE OF THE SHIFT in sentiment, the ebbing of citizen concern, the court continued to seek conspirators, still unsatisfied, if exhausted, growing increasingly weary of public opinion. The judiciary kept moving forward because that was its momentum, and, trusting nothing, could never believe any final resolution, more or less revelation, had in actuality been reached.

A new logical question was posed. If John Ury, the Papist spy, was so involved in the conspiracy, yet his existence brought so late to the attention of the courtroom, could there not be other, even larger fish, awaiting discovery?

After Ury's execution, pressure from politicos and slave-masters put pressure on the court to wrap up its case.

And the court took notice. Why were they doing that? Could it be that these individuals had something to hide? Could they be trying to stop the trial before it got close enough to uncover *them*?

So went the skewed logic of the last months. Could these higher-ups be guilty? Was it from them John Ury received his instruction?

You either had to continue with that paranoia and its perspective, or challenge the validity of all that had come before.

The ever-eager Mary Burton, called in response to these new suspicions, hinted that there were more at the top whom she had just happened to fail to mention before.

"I remember now, that there were white people of more than ordinary rank above the vulgar that were concerned," Mary gladly accommodated.

"What do you mean by this? Go on, Miss Burton, please. Make your statement, if any statement is to be made." Mary became silent in response, offering no more. Annoyed by this sudden uncooperative impertinence, the judges once more threatened her freedom and her life—and, of course, her promised hundred-pound reward. Mary, eager to remove herself from a precarious position once more, responded with further confessions.

"There were some people with ruffles that were concerned," Mary Burton told the hushed room.

Ruffles? That could only mean people better dressed than the ordinary, the clothing style of the upper class!

Threatened with the dungeon if she did not continue further, Mary Burton responded to the pressing judges, going on to name the only upper-class people she could think of, the only upper-class people she had ever come into contact with.

Mary Burton started naming the names of the family and associates of the very judges themselves.

The judges listened aghast as sweet little Mary now impeached those that they knew to be beyond suspicion and impeachment, astonished that their star witness, the one on whom the entire, prolonged case had rested, could lie so freely and easily, could besmirch the innocent in such casual manner. If Mary Burton was capable of this, what did that mean about the months of preceding testimony?

Shaken by this thunderbolt, the grand jury wrapped up that instant. The conspiracy case, in its entirey, was immediately closed. Before she could say another name (those that were said lastly being erased from the record and history completely), Mary Burton was proffered her money and promised freedom, putting an end to the investigation. The remaining slaves and whites in jail were either freed or quietly relocated before another question could be asked, or another answer created. The investigation into the Great Negro Plot was abruptly over. Everyone could go home now. There was nothing more to see here.

Of Mary Burton's final, libelous testimony, Daniel Horsmanden would himself years later rationalize that it comprised yet another attack by villains who intended with hindsight to discredit the proceedings in their entirety. Clearly, Horsmanden felt, that could be the only explanation. Still, although

Horsmanden felt thwarted, justice had to some degree been served, he insisted.

"A check has been put to the execrable malice, and bloody purposes of our foreign and domestic enemies, though we have not been able entirely to unravel the mystery of the iniquity; for it was a dark design, and the veil is in some measure still upon it!"

And there the veil would remain, lying in place to obscure the scrutiny of further generations.

In the city of New York the fear had dissipated, the context had changed. Once there had been great intoxication, and now there was the great and painful sobering that must follow. Awakening from their indulgence, rife with paranoia and racial distrust and hatred, the people of the city of New York felt their anxiety replaced with a greater peace, but also regret, and a greater shame.

In the end, both Caesar and John Hughson, if not in life, but in death, would be able to have their own final, posthumous word. It seems, in part, John Hughson's sign from the heaven would come. As their bodies remained hanging in public display all through the steaming New York summer of 1741 and into the fall of that year, the last two physical reminders of the court case that had so shaken the community for the months before, a miracle of sorts would happen. White in life, John Hughson's bloated, decomposing corpse would turn ebony black as it hung on view, darkened by its putrid rot. In contrast, the body of Caesar, enslaved in life, and brutalized because of its dark, melanin-rich skin, would decay, drain of blood, rot, and mold until its skin was nearly white to the eye. In death, the two maligned villains would trade the complexions that had been their burdens while living.

It was a sign, the colonists said, eyes transfixed on the aberration, as they kept walking apace, moving on with their lives now. God has spoken, they decided. Judgment had come.

BIBLIOGRAPHY

Books

Berlin, Ira, and Harris, Leslie M., eds. *Slavery in New York*. New York: New Press, 2005.

Burrows, Edwin G., and Wallace, Mike. *Gotham: A History of New York City to 1898*. New York: Oxford University Press, 1999.

Conniff, Michael L. *Africans in the Americas: A History of the Black Diaspora*. New York: St. Martin's Press, 1994.

Davis, Thomas J. *A Rumor of Revolt: The "Great Negro Plot" in Colonial New York*. Amherst: University of Massachusetts Press, 1990.

Foote, Thelma Wills. *Black and White Manhattan: The History of Racial Formation in Colonial New York City*. Oxford and New York: Oxford University Press, 2004.

Foote, Thelma Wills. *Black Life in Colonial Manhattan, 1664–1786*. Ph.D. thesis, Harvard University, 1991.

Goodwin, Maud Wilder. *Dutch and English on the Hudson: A Chronicle of Colonial New York*. New Haven: Yale University Press, 1921.

Hamlin, Paul. *Legal Education in Colonial New York*. New York: New York University Law Quarterly Review, 1939.

Harris, Leslie M. *In the Shadow of Slavery: African Americans in New York City, 1626–1863*. Chicago and London: University of Chicago Press, 2003.

Horsmanden, Daniel. *The New York Conspiracy*. Edited and with an introduction by Thomas J. Davis. Boston: Beacon Press, 1971.

Kammen, Michael G. *Colonial New York: A History*. New York: Oxford University Press, 1996.

Lepore, Jill. *New York Burning: Liberty, Slavery, and Conspiracy in Eighteenth-Century Manhattan*. New York: Knopf, 2005.

Articles

Blakey, M. L. "Skull Doctors: Intrinsic Social and Political Bias in the History of American Physical Anthropology." *Critique of Anthropology* 7, no. 2 (1987): 7–35.

Blakey, Michael L., and R. C. Vargui. "A Comparison of Dental Enamel Defects in Christian and Meroitic Populations from Geili, Central Sudan." *International Journal of Anthropology* 5, no. 3 (1990).

Blakey, Michael L. "The New York African Burial Ground Project: An Examination of Enslaved Lives, a Construction of Ancestral Ties." *Transforming Anthropology* 7, no. 1 (1998): 53–58.

Bower, Beth A. "Material Culture in Boston: The Black Experience." In *The Archaeology of Inequality*, edited by Randall H. McGuire and Robert Paynter, 55–63. Cambridge, Mass.: Basil Blackwell, 1991.

Davis, Thomas. "Slavery in Colonial New York City." Ann Arbor, Mich.: University Microfilms International, 1981.

Davis, Thomas J. "These Enemies of Their Own Household: A Note on the Troublesome Slave Population in Eighteenth Century New York City." In *Articles on American Slavery: Slavery in the North and West*, vol. 5, edited by Paul Finkelman, 17–37. New York: Garland Press, 1989.

LaRoche, Cheryl J. "Beads from the African Burial Ground, New York City: A Preliminary Assessment." *Beads: Journal of the Society of Bead Researchers* 6 (1994): 3–20.

Perry, Warren R., and Michael L. Blakey. "Archaeology as Community Service: the African Burial Ground Project in New York City." In *Lessons from the Past: An Introductory Reader in Archaeology*, 45–51. Mountain View, Calif.: Mayfield Publishing, 1999.

A NOTE ON THE AUTHOR

Mat Johnson is the author of the novels *Hunting in Harlem* and *Drop*. He received his M.F.A. from Columbia and now teaches at Bard College. He lives in New York's Hudson Valley with his family.